Chemical and Biological Defence at Porton Down 1916-2000

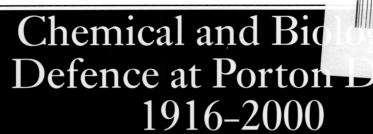

by

G B CARTER ISO

2000

London: The Stationery Office

First published 2000

ISBN 0 11 772933 7

Published by The Stationery Office and available from:

The Stationery Office
(mail, telephone and fax orders only)
PO Box 29, Norwich, NR3 1GN
Telephone orders/General enquiries 0870 600 5522
Fax orders 0870 600 5533

www.ukstate.com

The Stationery Office Bookshops
123 Kingsway, London WC2B 6PQ
020 7242 6393 Fax 020 7242 6412
68–69 Bull Street, Birmingham B4 6AD
0121 236 9696 Fax 0121 236 9699
33 Wine Street, Bristol BS1 2BQ
0117 926 4306 Fax 0117 929 4515
9–21 Princess Street, Manchester M60 8AS
0161 834 7201 Fax 0161 833 0634
16 Arthur Street, Belfast BT1 4GD
028 9023 8451 Fax 028 9023 5401
The Stationery Office Oriel Bookshop
18–19 High Street, Cardiff CF1 2BZ
029 2039 5548 Fax 029 2038 4347
71 Lothian Road, Edinburgh EH3 9AZ
0870 606 5566 Fax 0870 606 5588

The Stationery Office's Accredited Agents
(see Yellow Pages)

and through good booksellers

Contents

Foreword

By Professor Sir Keith O'Nions FRS, Chief Scientific Adviser to the Ministry of Defence

Defence research has been undertaken at Porton Down for more than 80 years, although its activities and role in UK defence has evolved over this period. Since the late 1950s its central role has been to ensure that the United Kingdom Armed Forces are provided with effective protective measures against the threats posed by chemical and biological weapons. The fruits of some of the outstanding research were realised during the Gulf conflict of late 1990 and early 1991 and more recently to support further operations in the Gulf region.

The technical challenge to provide protection against the diverse threat posed by chemical and biological weapons is very great indeed. A programme of research to meet this need must inevitably span a wide range of requirements including, amongst others, an in-depth understanding of the hazard that UK Armed Forces might encounter; detecting and identifying as rapidly as possible what has been used; collating and disseminating information to warn friendly forces of an attack; providing physical protection such as suits and respirators, as well as collective protection; minimising contamination; and investigating the use of medical countermeasures such as vaccines. Porton Down has risen to the challenges and built a multi-disciplinary team of experts who seek innovative solutions to the problems posed. They operate at the highest standards of scientific excellence and provide MOD with integrated technical advice to support equipment procurement, military doctrine and policy-making.

At present CBD Sector at Porton, as part of the Defence Evaluation and Research Agency, employs some 700 staff and has readily embraced the new technologies of the era including all the benefits that biotechnology may bring to providing effective protection to our servicemen and women.

Porton provides a range of support across several Government departments. It continues a play an important role in arms control, supporting the UK delegation in Geneva on a Protocol to strengthen compliance with the 1972 Biological and Toxin Weapons Convention. Furthermore it actively supports the UK's obligations under the 1993 Chemical Weapons Convention.

In the year 2000, I feel that we should reflect on the achievements at Porton Down over the last 84 years. Visiting Porton today you will see a thriving scientific establishment with an eye to the future. New facilities will open shortly, providing the most up-to-date laboratory containment suites in Europe for the safe handling of pathogenic micro-organisms. Furthermore, a budding Science Park is now hosted on the site and aims to foster a cluster of biotechnology expertise that is developing in South Wiltshire.

Unfortunately the threat from chemical and biological weapons remains undiminished and continues to pose challenges for Governments in this new century. Ensuring that our scientific understanding of chemical and biological weapons and the means to mitigate their effects will be as important as ever. I am sure that CBD Porton Down will continue to serve us exceptionally well in this role.

Acknowledgements

Several people in the CBD Sector have provided input for this book; I am most grateful to them for discussions. I am particularly grateful to Barbara Prince for word processing.

The Headquarters building at the CBD Sector, built by the Royal Engineers in 1918 and now a listed building.

A Note About the Author

G B Carter, ISO CBiol MIBIOL

Gradon Carter joined the Ministry of Supply's Microbiological Research Department at Porton Down in 1948, working in experimental pathology, virology and the administration of research until 1976 when he went for three and a half years to the Ministry of Defence's Directorate of Scientific and Technical Intelligence. He returned to Porton's Chemical Defence Establishment in 1979, working in its Medical Division and then headed the Technical Intelligence and Information Section until his first retirement in 1990. For the next five years he worked on information research, finally retiring from full-time service in 1995. Since then he has been a part-time consultant on historical topics at the CBD Sector. His earlier publications in scientific journals and texts reflect past interests in rapid laboratory identification of viruses and the pathology of experimental air-borne infection. Fourteen later publications, both individual and conjoint, are on historical aspects of chemical and biological warfare and on Porton Down. In 1992 Her Majesty's Stationery Office published his 'Porton Down: 75 years of chemical and biological research', the precursor to this present book.

Introduction

In the year 2000, it is eighty four years since the establishment of the hutted laboratories and the associated "experimental ground" on Porton Down in 1916 to study chemical warfare and soon afterwards, chemical defence. The "experimental ground" was set up in response to the first use of gas by the German Army. By 1915, the first retaliatory attacks by the British Army had already been made and had brought the realisation that chemical warfare had to be based on data scientifically derived by practical experiment in the field under controlled conditions and not be based wholly on ad hoc observations of what happened under operational conditions on the battlefield. Whilst some initial field trials took place on Clapham Common, at Crewe, Runcorn, Cannock Chase and elsewhere in the United Kingdom, as well as in France at the village of Helfaut, most of the development of operational use sprang from little else beyond such use and observations. By early 1916, the need for a United Kingdom based field trials area had been identified and eventually a suitable site at Porton was selected. The year 2000 also sees the sixtieth anniversary of the setting up of a group at Porton during the Second World War to study the methods of biological warfare in response to the threat of Axis powers using this then unknown and largely unstudied method of war.

This book summarises eighty four years of Porton's preoccupation with chemical matters and sixty years of activity in microbiological matters. It is intended to be intelligible to a diverse readership with many differing levels of knowledge about chemical and biological warfare and varying familiarity with Porton, as well as being of interest to any other reader. It will also provide an account of the history of Porton for the present staff of the two quite distinct establishments, the Chemical and Biological Defence (CBD) Sector and the Centre for Applied Microbiology and Research (CAMR).

Given that over 80 years have elapsed since work started, there is a paucity of well known openly available literature on the history of activities at Porton. The first such major account is the Commandant's 1919 report on Porton during the Great War of 1914–1918: this document, known as the "Crossley Report" is now in the Public Records Office, together with several thousand earlier reports from Porton. The second major work is the 1960 "A

History of Porton" by an old Portonian, Lieutenant Colonel A E Kent, covering the period from 1916–1960. Known as "Kent's History", it has recently been deposited in the Public Records Office, It was abridged in 1960 and this shortened version was published as a Restricted booklet in 1961 entitle "A Brief History of the Chemical Defence Experimental Establishment, Porton". It was de-classified to unlimited status in 1987 and put in the Public Records Office. Its author was C G Trotman, although this fact is not recorded in the booklet.

None of these three texts were intended for public readership. Traditionally, public or even parliamentary curiosity about chemical and biological warfare was not encouraged in the United Kingdom. Until comparatively recent times, little need was seen for positive public relations activity, although the late 1960s saw a massive series of press and public visits to Open Days at both the Porton establishments. Things changed slightly in 1955 when the Director of the Microbiological Research Establishment published an account of the Establishment's research in the Proceedings of the Royal Society, as did the successive Director, Dr C E Gordon Smith in the journal Chemistry and Industry in 1967, but it was not really until the 90s that the senior Porton Establishment moved emphatically under Dr G S Pearson into producing openly available accounts of the history of Porton Down and the United Kingdom's past and present policies.

In 1991 thought was directed to how best the then Chemical and Biological Defence Establishment's 75th Anniversary should be celebrated. It was finally decided that an illustrated book intended for public readers would fulfil requirements. Accordingly, the 1992 HMSO publication "Porton Down: 75 Years of Chemical and Biological Research" was written. Since then 2,000 copies have been distributed by the former Chemical and Biological Defence Establishment or sold by the former HMSO: the book is now out of print.

This present book is its replacement. It is not a reprint, nor a new edition, nor a completely new book It does, however, reflect the increased transparency of recent times about the United Kingdom's past activities in chemical and biological warfare and defence to a degree which was seen as not possible in an earlier period and provides insight into the activity of the last eight years at Porton Down.

Any account of Porton's past is interwoven with the sometimes complex history of chemical and biological warfare. Chemical and biological warfare have, in the past, been seen as quite separate entities for some purposes: at other times they have been much interwoven and they have many similarities. Many readers may therefore be helped by the inclusion of an appendix on the nature of chemical and biological warfare, and on arms control. One further clarification may be helpful: this booklet is not about a single Porton Establishment but largely about two distinct entities, albeit that for a decade they were co-located and for a further near three decades, adjacent. As far as possible the descriptions of events and activities in this booklet use the titles which were extant at the time: where no ambiguity arises, the term Sector, Establishment or Porton is used. The media have traditionally failed to discriminate between the several bodies and Establishments at Porton: this is not surprising because there are complex aspects of Porton. For most of the past Porton has had two and briefly three distinct defence Establishments. These were all once a part of a large Directorate with a London-based headquarters and further outposts at Sutton Oak and later Nancekuke. Staff passed back and forth between the outposts and the headquarters and sometimes also to India, Australia and Canada. Some clarification emerges if the successive titles for the major establishments at Porton are set out chronologically.

Titles for the chemical warfare or chemical defence and the subsequent chemical and biological defence area

War Department Experimental Ground	1916
Royal Engineers Experimental Station	1916–1929[1]
Chemical Warfare Experimental Station (CWES)	1929–1930[1]
Chemical Defence Experimental Station (CDES)	1930–1948[1]
Chemical Defence Experimental Establishment (CDEE)	1948–1970
Chemical Defence Establishment (CDE)	1970–1991
Chemical and Biological Defence Establishment (CBDE)	1991–1995
Chemical and Biological Defence (CBD) Sector of the Defence Evaluation and Research Agency (DERA)	1995–

---

[1]   In such times many official papers used merely the title.

Titles for the biological warfare or biological defence areas

Biology Department, Porton (BDP)	1940–1946[2]
Microbiological Research Department (MRD)	1946–1957[3]
Microbiological Research Establishment (MRE)	1957–1979[4]

In 1979, when the Microbiological Research Establishment closed, the then CDE became responsible for both chemical and biological defence.

The former MRE building became the Centre for Applied Microbiology and Research (CAMR) in 1979 as part of the Public Health Laboratory Service (PHLS) within the Department of Health and unconnected with the Ministry of Defence. Later, in 1994, the Microbiological Research Authority (MRA) was formed as a Special Health Authority by statutory instrument under the National Health Service Act of 1977. CAMR became a constituent part of the MRA, reporting through its Board and the Department of Health to the Secretary of State for Health and abandoned its affiliation to the PHLS. This book does not deal with CAMR and its owners after April 1979. The 2000 text by Hammond and Carter continues the history of microbiology at CAMR (see the bibliography). Accounts of microbiology in the defence field at CDE, CBDE and the CBD Sector of DERA from April 1979 continue in earlier papers and in this book.

Finally, there was at one time a separate Porton Establishment known generally as the Farm. The present animal breeding unit and the farm comprised from 1949–1973 a distinct Establishment of successively the Ministry of Supply, the War Department and the Ministry of Defence, known as Animal Farm, Porton and from 1954 as Allington Farm, Porton and with its own Superintendent. In 1973 Allington Farm became part of the then CDE. At one time the title Animal Farm was used instead of Allington Farm. During the Second World War the supply of animals from Allington Farm was the responsibility of the Royal Army Veterinary Corps and the farm was briefly known as the Zoology Section.

---

[2]   Located within the then CDES but as an autonomous unit.

[3]   Located initially within CDES as described about (2) but from 1951 as a geographically separate Establishment with a mile of CDES.

[4]   Merely a change of title.

The Beginning:
The Great War of 1914–1918

1

Before the Great War, the Porton area was relatively untouched by the military activities which later spread over much of southern Wiltshire and especially Salisbury Plain, though on 8 September 1898, 50,000 troops assembled at Porton Down and marched to a review at Boscombe Down; an activity over then private land enabled by the recent Military Manoeuvres Act of 1887. Porton Down was not part of Salisbury Plain and was separated from it by the railway. The owners of land at Porton were numerous and seemingly ever-changing: they included Lord Normanton, Lord Nelson, the Countess of Portsmouth, Sir Harry Malet of Wilbury House, the Eyre-Matchams and many others. A few cottages, barns, farm buildings and, to the south, smallholdings were scattered over the chalk downs and the plantations. The only house of any size was "Old Lodge", a 17th Century farmstead much restored in mid-Victorian days as a home for the Poore family and located four miles west of Nether Wallop.

The Poores were descendants of the family of Bishop Poore, who founded Salisbury cathedral in the 13th Century. Major Robert Poore was a prosperous and sporting country gentleman with a large family and an enlightened attitude to the conditions of

Old Lodge at some unknown time in the late years of last century. This pleasant early Victorian house of brick and flint was probably built on the site of a 17th century keepers lodge. When Major Poore moved in during the 1870s he demolished a chapel at the house and extensively enlarged the house to provide a gymnasium, Turkish bath and a laundry. It is unclear why the house was not used as accommodation or laboratories by the army in 1916. Reputedly, it soon fell into decay and was at times occupied by gypsies. until it was demolished in 1924 or 1925.

the Wiltshire farm worker. He had fought in India with the 8th Hussars and retired from the Army in 1864. He was responsible for the famous Winterslow Land Court which brought a form of local government before the Parish Council Act of 1895 and enabled the ownership of small plots. He became a Wiltshire County Councillor and Justice of the Peace. Mrs Poore was one of the founders of the now defunct Winterslow Weaving Industry, later to become the Stonehenge Woollen Industries. All their seven children are described as "marrying-well", usually into the nobility of the era. Perhaps the most unusual was Nina, the youngest, who became Duchess of Hamilton and Brandon: she devoted her life to animal welfare and founded the Ferne Animal Sanctuary at one of the ducal houses, Ferne House near Berwick St John. In later life she became the constant companion of the eccentric Admiral of the Fleet Lord Fisher, whilst her invalid husband, the premier peer of Scotland, pursued a quiet life.

Events on the Western Front in 1915 were to bring great changes to the Poores and to the tranquil rural life of Porton. On 22 April, the Algerian Division of the French Army was attacked at Ypres, when the Germans discharged about 150 tons of chlorine from 6000 emplaced cylinders over a front of nearly four miles. The effects were devastating. Those who were not suffocated, quickly broke from their lines and fled; the front collapsed. On 24 April the now uncovered flank of the 2nd Canadian Brigade was similarly attacked. The first British troops to experience German "gas" were the 1st Battalion of the Dorset Regiment on 1 May. On 23 April, Sir John French the British Commander-in-Chief reported the first German attack on the French troops and urged the War Office that "Immediate steps be taken to supply similar means of most effective kind for use by our troops". Retaliation-in-kind and the means of defence were immediate needs: Sir John also signalled "Also essential that our troops should be immediately provided with means of countering enemy gases".

The complexity of the subsequent British and Allied reaction involved many areas beyond Porton Down, such as the chemical industry, the Ministry of Munitions, the Royal Society and the Services. Defensive matters were largely the concern of the Anti-Gas Department in London, located mainly at the Royal Army Medical College until May 1917. The matter of retaliation was initially allotted to the Scientific Advisory Committee of the Ministry of Munitions. Consideration of which gas might be used by Britain was constrained both by industrial capabilities and the lack of a suitable area for tests on a realistic scale. Some cylinders were discharged in a trial on 4 June at the Castner Kellner works at

Runcorn and the first British consignment of chlorine was sent to France on 10 July 1915. The first British retaliatory gas attack was at Loos on 25 September 1915. The charging of agents into shell and grenades and Service requirements were also discussed but it became clear that the reality of an effective British response awaited a scientific approach. In September 1915 the Director General of the Trench Warfare Department nominated an officer to serve his Department's new Scientific Advisory committee by finding a suitable "ground for experimental purposes". Many sites were visited; in the interim some trials involving the discharge of hydrogen sulphide from cylinders had been done at Cannock Chase in December 1915.

Sites in Dorset, Suffolk, Hampshire and Wiltshire, including some in the neighbourhood of Andover, Netheravon, Stonehenge and Porton were visited by Professor H B Baker FRS, and then on 9 January 1916 by other members of the Committee. They recommended that steps be taken to acquire the Porton site and in the next few months an initial 2886 acres of the land near Porton was acquired from several of the owners. By 1918, further necessary extensions had resulted in the acquisition of Old Lodge and areas to the north-east and east, and the creation of Porton South (in the area now occupied by the Defence NBC Centre at Winterbourne Gunner) to a total of 6196 acres with a further separate 310 acres on the north side of the Amesbury and Military Camp Light Railway at Arundel Farm, a few miles west of Newton Tony.

The site was first described as "The War Department Experimental Ground, Porton": the appellation of Porton has remained though the site is rather nearer to the village of Idmiston and Idmiston Down. In the years before the existence of a road (constructed in 1924–1925) between Porton village and the London road, the main entrance to the Establishment was at the Idmiston railway bridge. Later in 1916, the title "Royal Engineers Experimental Station, Porton" was adopted, reflecting the contemporary dominance of the Royal Engineers in British chemical warfare. On 7 March 1916 Sergeant Major Dobbs of the Royal Engineers reported for duty at the Experimental Ground. It is not clear whether there was anyone at Porton to report to; possibly he actually reported to the headquarters of Southern Command (which was then at Radnor House in Salisbury, on the site now largely occupied by the roundabout at the junction of the Wilton and Devizes roads) before taking the train or being driven out to Porton. On 16 March notification was received that 100 industrial-type cylinders containing hydrogen sulphide had been prepared at Oldbury, Birmingham under the supervision of Professor John Cadman of Birmingham University, a member of the Chemical Sub-Committee of the Scientific Advisory Committee of the Ministry of Munitions. After being transported by rail from Birmingham the cylinders (circa 5 feet long, 8 inches in diameter and weighing when full nearly 60 kilogrammes) were moved from Porton railway station to the experimental ground by local civilian labour, a slow and difficult process on account of the absence of proper roads. The cylinders were stored in what became known as "Gas Wood" near the central bowl of the range and a night watchman was engaged to guard them.

Two large army huts had arrived on the ground on 30 March, one for an office and the other for a store. At the time it was thought that these were all the huts that would be needed at Porton but by May the Chemical Advisory Committee (formerly the Scientific Advisory Committee) of the Trench Warfare Research Department presented its view that the Porton ground should be put on a more effective basis and that £4000 should be spent on roads, fencing and workshops. Meanwhile, Sergeant Major Dobbs had been joined by Lieutenant Murray of the Royal Engineers as Officer in Charge of Works, to supervise constructions by the gang of thirty workmen; a body which may be seen as the forerunner of the Porton Works Department, the Ministry of Works, and later the Property Services Agency; branches which have looked after the fabric of the Porton campus over the years. Such work only proceeded rapidly from January 1917 and electric power, a light railway and considerable workshops and general facilities were available by 1918. At the time of the Armistice in 1918, what is now called the Headquarters or Main Block was under construction as the administration building; plans for more permanent buildings were also being considered.

On 6 April 1916 six civilians trained in the use of the "Proto" self-contained breathing sets from the mine rescue team at Hednesford, Staffordshire arrived at Porton: they were to take samples of gas clouds as they passed from the point of discharge. On 11 April thirteen civilian workmen were "sworn under the Official Secrets Act" to be trained by Sergeant Major Dobbs in opening the hydrogen sulphide cylinders. An open air laboratory for analysis of gas samples was set up in the corner of "Gas Wood". However, the weather remained unsuitable for several weeks with both the mine rescue team and the Committee being summoned and returning to their homes on several occasions. In the interim a few desultory experiments were done on the flammability of hydrogen sulphide and the effect of explosives on cylinders. A

Professor Walker also sprayed chloropicrin from a cylinder by means of compressed air. However, the major experiment with 120 cylinders of hydrogen sulphide finally took place on 26 May 1916, when the gas was released over a hundred yards front upwind of a system of trenches. Rats in cages were exposed in these and in the open. The mine rescue team, protected by their self-contained breathing apparatus, sampled the cloud as it passed over them by opening previously emplaced evacuated Winchester quart bottles. The trial was successful in that lethal concentrations were demonstrated at least 300 yards from the point of release.

However, British interest in hydrogen sulphide was short-lived. Though lethal, it was dangerously flammable, corrosive to cylinders, too light to stay near the ground after release and possessed a distinctive smell at very low concentration, enabling early awareness of its presence. A mixture of hydrogen sulphide and chloropicrin was more acceptable; this was heavier and not so readily dissipated. This mixture, known as "Green Star" was stockpiled in France in 1916 with the aim of a future surprise attack on a vast scale. In the interim about 75% of the cylinders corroded and "Green Star" was all but abandoned as a chemical agent by July 1917.

The "Proto" team sent from Porton to the mine rescue training centre at Hednesford near Cannock for training in the use of oxygen-breathing apparatus. Their names were (back row, left to right) Harding, Adams, Morgan, Robertshaw and (front row) McMerry, Eames and James. Eventually after their role in field trials, all these men except McMerry worked in the laboratories at Porton. The Chemical Defence Experimental Establishment was sent this photograph by Mr Adams in 1968.

The use of chemical warfare in the field was seen as a suitable new role for the Royal Engineers. Initially, four "Special Companies" (so called to conceal their actual nature) were raised in France by the posting of suitable soldiers from other units, and men with scientific experience or qualifications, who were to be enlisted as corporals with special rates of pay. Major (later Major General) C H Foulkes Royal Engineers, was promoted to Lieutenant Colonel and was appointed Gas Advisor to the Commander-in-Chief of the British Expeditionary Force in France and Commander of what was to evolve into the Royal Engineers "Special Brigade". The first draft of two officers and eighty men reached Foulkes at St Omer on 18 July 1915; more appeared on 21 July. An experimental ground was set up at Helfaut and training commenced in meteorology, theory and the practicalities of gas cylinder deployment. Despite great problems in production of chlorine and the supply of cylinders, the stockpile grew. On 22 August a demonstration was given to twenty or thirty of the senior Generals of the British Expeditionary Force. The first British attack was by now fixed for 15 September. On 4 September 1915 the Special Companies that had finished training moved up to the front at Loos; all wore brassards of pink, white and green, colours which were perpetuated until 1979 at Porton in the mess tie. The battle was however postponed; in the interim some 5500 cylinders were emplaced. At

5.50 am on 25 September gas and smoke were released from the emplacements to roll steadily towards the German lines. Britain's retaliatory capability had been demonstrated within five months of the first German use of gas on the Western Front. However, the Germans were by now moving towards shells containing chemical agents, giving greater precision and flexibility: Britain too needed to progress beyond emplaced cylinders. Despite some scope for experiments in the field in France, it was clear that real progress would not be made by Britain until options were properly evaluated by scientific means. Such evaluations at Porton started in May 1916 and continued intensively. The results of trials and studies during the Great War at Porton were reported mainly by the publication of 7798 reports under the aegis of the Colonel Commandant Porton: these are now in the Public Record Office at Kew.

Foulkes was not a Porton man. He was offered and declined the post of Commandant at Porton after the war, but in 1919 he became a member of the Holland Committee which made profound recommendations on the future of chemical warfare and of Porton. Foulkes continued to serve in the Royal Engineers and returned briefly in his retirement to serve on the Weapons Committee of the Chemical Defence Board during the Second World War. He died in 1969 in his 95th year, doyen of the Colonels Commandant of his regiment and also father of a Colonel Commandant.

The outstanding figure at Porton during the Great War was its Commandant, Lieutenant Colonel A W Crossley FRS. Before 1916, Arthur Crossley, a Mancunian, as Professor of Organic Chemistry at Kings College, London, had been a distinguished academic and chemist, drawn into war work under the aegis of the Royal Society, initially as Secretary of the Chemical Sub-Committee of the Royal Society's War Committee, and then of the Scientific Advisory Committee of the Ministry of Munitions. In June 1916 Crossley was appointed to the post of Commandant and Superintendent of Experiments at Porton. He had been appointed Liaison Officer for Chemical Warfare, with the rank of Lieutenant Colonel in November 1915 and had spent some time in France. When Crossley arrived at Porton he found Sergeant Major Dobbs and Lieutenant Murray, two army huts with no roads leading to them, no water and no equipment. Within the month a chemistry laboratory was active in one of the huts: from the moment Crossley arrived work was done all day and most of the night.

In 1918, after the Armistice, Arthur Crossley was appointed Daniell Professor of Chemistry at Kings College and retired to the college on demobilisation in October 1919. In 1920 he turned to

Lieutenant Colonel A W Crossley CMG DSc LLD FRS RE in 1918 painted by Lieutenant C A C Stainer RGA and presented to Crossley by his fellow officers at Porton.

organising the British Cotton Industry Research Association at what is now the Shirley Institute in Didsbury. He received many honours from the State, the Royal Society and the Chemical Society before he died in 1927. The octagonal entrance hall to the headquarters block at the Sector has a brass memorial to Crossley; this was placed originally in the long-demolished hutted church at the Establishment. A portrait of Crossley painted by Lieutenant C A C Stainer of the Royal Garrison Artillery, stationed at Porton during the Great War as the official "artist", hangs in the Headquarters Building Main Conference Room together with Crossley's LL.D hood and his D.Sc gown and hood. The painting was presented to Crossley in April 1918 as a mark of the esteem in which he was held by his fellow officers at Porton: their signatures are on a commemorative address pasted to the back of the frame.

There can now be few soldiers or civilians still alive who served at Porton during the Great War: our impressions of that period in the history of the Establishment come mainly from the "Crossley Report". Crossley was a keen photographer and the "Crossley Report" is augmented by three large albums of half-plate photographs showing many facets of life at Porton under his command. These albums were presented to the Establishment by the Crossley family in later years.

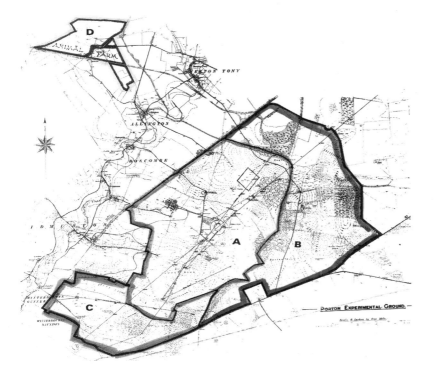

A map from the 1919 "Crossley Report" showing the four stages in the acquisition of the experimental ground: first the red, then successively the green, blue and yellow-banded areas.

Crossley tells us that up to July 1916, civilian "workmen" had been used extensively for experimental work, but on 5 July a detachment of nine NCOs and thirteen men of the Special Brigade Royal Engineers arrived as the nucleus of an experimental party. On arrival from Chatham at Porton Railway Station they were met by the military foreman of works and the village constable. Half the detachment were billeted by the constable in railway cottages and the rest in Idmiston village. The detachment paraded each morning at Idmiston church and marched up the cart track to the Experimental Ground. In September 1916 a series of major discharges from cylinders took place to optimise the techniques of sampling and analysing the cloud. As work progressed, and as German use of chemical warfare embraced the use of chemical shell rather than solely cylinders, it became obvious that experiments using artillery would have to be initiated. A special detachment of the Royal Artillery from Shoeburyness were used initially for this work, which started on 21 July 1916 with the firing of 4.5" howitzer shells charged with SK(ethyl iodoacetate; a powerful and one time standard British lachrymator named after South Kensington, where laboratory experiments were first done; probably at Imperial College) into "Gas Wood" from what is now known as Battery Hill (then more usually known as Spion Kop because a private bungalow so named was earlier located there). Initial activity by the detachment had revealed inadequacies and the recommendation was made that a permanent artillery unit be made available. Accordingly, in February 1917 the nucleus of what

One of the few surviving photographs from the Great War showing a workshop dealing with respirators.

was to become the Porton Battery Royal Artillery arrived, with the two-fold role of firing for experimental trials and for the proofing of gas shell. The tradition of a Royal Artillery presence at Porton continued until 1957, when the Battery was disbanded.

The "Crossley Report" describes the work of the Station in great detail, the way in which it was administered and the diverse engineering and allied facilities which gradually arose. For instance we read that, at the time of the Armistice, in the Motor Transport Section there were thirteen touring cars, eight Ford vans, four 15 cwt lorries, four 13 cwt lorries; ten steam lorries, nine motor-bicycles, two ambulances, two charabancs and a wagonette. Horsed transport also abounded. The Porton Light Railway, a 24 inch gauge system, had five steam locomotives, one petrol locomotive and 150 carriages and wagons of several sorts. The railway started at sidings alongside the London and South Western Railway Company main line at Porton station and its eight miles of track ramified throughout the Station, the ranges and later to Porton South. The carriage of civilian workmen and fuel and stores to and from the main line Porton Station was a major role; it being the principal route for civilian labour from Salisbury. The light railway was still in use in 1951, though by that time the steam locomotives had gone. The Porton Light Railway, also known as the Porton Military Railway, was a notable feature. By the 1950s it threaded its way to every major building on the site. When the new Microbiological Research Department, later the Microbiological Research Establishment and now the Centre for Applied Microbiology and Research, was being built in 1948–1951, a temporary extension of the railway was built parallel with and to the south of the building for the transport of building materials to the site. The disappearance of the Porton Light Railway is almost completely and woefully unrecorded. It seems to have been phased out in the mid-1950s. There is no information on the disposal of the rolling stock. One length of rail survives set in concrete within the Sector's Enclosed Area and some rail plates survive in an overgrown cutting but essentially this once complex system is no

Porton from the South in March 1918: construction had not yet started on the Headquarters Building; agriculture and road making are seen in the foreground.

The light railway constructed during the Great War of 1914–1918 at Porton is of great interest to military railway enthusiasts. Its main original purpose was to provide a link with the London and South Western Railway main line at Porton Station for the conveyance of workmen and stores to Porton Camp. When the two feet gauge line got to Porton Camp it split into a considerable network of branches and sidings to serve most areas of the camp and range: a line also extended to South Camp, now the Defence NBC Centre at Winterbourne Gunner. Coal, oil, munitions, timber and building materials could be readily distributed. The light railway gradually became less important and by the mid-1950s had ceased to exist. The track was eventually taken up but most of the original route can still be traced.

more. Military railway enthusiasts should see the paper by K P Norris listed in the first bibliography.

Because of the food shortage, agricultural activity was started on the Station in 1917. One of the earliest British sugar beet crops was produced: corn, root and hay were also produced for fodder for the experimental animals. Animals were originally accommodated at Porton Down Barn (at the foot of the present road from the "Porton-Pheasant road" to Battery Hill). Unfortunately the noise of the guns on Battery Hill was found to interfere with the breeding of some species and a new 314 acre animal farm was started at Arundel Farm, beyond the boundary of the Station and a few miles west of Newton Toney. Goats were much used for experimental work since their respiratory volume resembled that of man; in 1918 some 560 were housed at the new farm. Medical and toxicological work became of increasing importance as the war progressed. Data on the lethality of gas in relation to both concentration and period of exposure were critical to a proper understanding of gas poisoning and its treatment. Many toxic substances were examined; some 147 are recorded as having been studied at Porton before the Armistice.

The first physiological laboratory was set up in the main camp in 1917 but was later moved to Boscombe Down Farm on the Range and much enlarged, only to be burned down in the summer of 1917 and replaced by several hutted laboratories. Mr Barcroft (later Sir Joseph Barcroft), the physiologist, was eventually assisted by Captain R A Peters RAMC (later Sir Rudolph Peters) who had experience of gas casualties in France. Other RAMC personnel were attached for special duties in the treatment of gas poisoning and to establish liaison with medical officers at casualty clearing stations and base hospitals. When the Anti-Gas Department from the Royal Army Medical College moved to Porton in 1917, co-operation with

The Royal Automobile Club Section at Porton: public-spirited car owners donned uniform to serve the Army. The windscreen of the central car carries the message "RAC on war service".

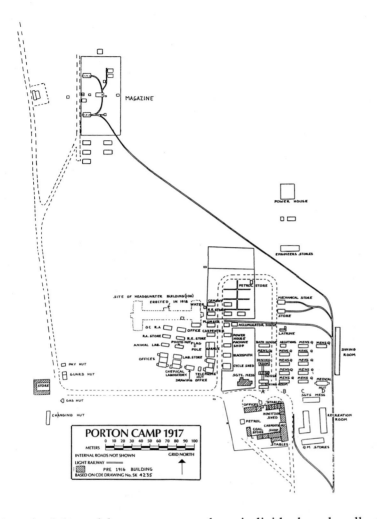

Porton Camp in 1917.
The hatched buildings are those cottages and farm buildings which existed on the site before the army came to Porton.

the physiology laboratory to explore individual and collective protection against gas because of great importance. This work was largely done by the then Captain H Hartley who was later appointed Controller of the Chemical Warfare Department at the War Office in November 1918 and, as Sir Harold Hartley, retained links with chemical warfare and defence virtually until his death in 1972.

Crossley describes how the work of the several departments was integrated, such as when an artillery experiment was designed to compare the lethality of the same gas fired from guns with different calibres required the involvement of the chemical laboratory to take and analyse samples, the physiological laboratory to provide and monitor experimental animals and to report on the clinical effects and pathology of the gas, the meteorological section, the Experimental Battery Royal Artillery for charging and firing of munitions, the Experimental Company Royal Engineers for trials organisation and layout and the deployment of volunteer observers, and the draughtsmen for observing and recording the fall of shell. Much use was made of the human observer who was unmasked but with his respirator at the ready, to act as the ultimate sensor and recorder of the effects on man.

Whilst much energy was devoted to offensive aspects of chemical warfare, the protection of the British soldier was a no less important matter. The first Anti-Gas Departments had been in London at the Royal Army Medical College and later at University College. Studies were also done at Bedford College, the Lister Institute, the Physiology Laboratories of Oxford University and the Central Laboratory in France. Following the first gas attacks, the immediate need was for the provision of gas masks (or "respirators" as they became known).

Within 36 hours of the first use of gas against the French

May 1915 The Black Veil Respirator
This was the first official protection issued to British troops in France after the first gas attack by the Germans. The black gauge veiling contained cotton waste soaked in a solution of sodium thiosulphate (the photographers "hypo"), washing soda and glycerine and gave protection against low concentrations of chlorine. The veil was a temporary expedient and by May 1915 a better device was available.

May 1915 The "H" (hypo) Helmet
This was designed at the Royal Army Medical College, Millbank by a team under Colonel W H Horrocks RAMC. It was little more than a flannel bag impregnated with a hypo solution, with a big talc window.

January 1916 The "PH" Helemet
In 1915 it was found that hexamine was an admirable absorbent of phosgene. From 20 January 1916 all "P" helmets were impregnated with both sodium phenate and hexamine and were known as "PH" Helmets.

forces, an improvised mouth-pad of some sort had been issued to all British troops. Improved impregnated pads or "veils" such as the Haldane cotton waste-thiosulphate respirator followed in the early summer of 1915 but clearly the pad or "veil" had limited utility. The idea of an impregnated flannel helmet with a mica window

January 1916 The PHG Helmet
These were "PH" helmets with goggles to give protection against tear gas to gunners. Few were issued since the box respirators was being introduced.

1915–1916 The "Large Box or "Tower" Respirator
This was devised by Sergeant (later Lieutenant Colonel) E F Harrison, in peacetime a chemist with many industrial contacts, at the Royal Army Medical College, Anti-gas Department. (The earlier helmets were limited by the degree to which protection could be afforded against a wide range of different gases. Also, fabric was not an ideal surface on which to support chemical absorbents. It seemed better to arrange a gas mask where the air was drawn through a box or canister containing absorbent. In 1915 Mr B Lambert of Oxford University tested granules of lime and sodium permanganate within a simple box and the foundation of the respirator canister was laid).
The "Large Box" respirator canister contained a range of absorbents, including charcoal. It was held in a haversack and connected to the facepiece and a metal tube held in the mouth. The nostrils were closed by a metal clip and a pair of goggles completed the equipment. The "Large Box" respirator gave a very high degree of protection but was unnecessarily large for ordinary use in the field.

June 1916 The "Small Box" Respirator
This appeared in 1916 as a general issue and was thereafter the standard issue through the Great War. The facepiece incorporated celluloid eyepieces. Later a canister extension and then a new canister was produced to give protection against airborne toxic particles and glass eyepieces replace those of celluloid.

(the "Hypo" helmet) was conceived, followed by the Phenate helmet and the Phenate-Hexamine helmet. Goggles were also produced to complement some devices. The more efficient and comfortable concept of an impervious facepiece with eyepieces and the essential gas adsorbents and filters incorporated in an attached container soon arose. It had the merit that any necessary specific absorbents for new gases could be added as a further layer in the container, a method not feasible with a fabric helmet The first or "Large Box" respirator issued in August 1916 had a container holding soda lime-permanganate granules, a facepiece of proofed fabric, mouthpiece, nose-clip and separate goggles. The facepiece was connected to the "box" by a rubber tube. As with most respirators, numerous continuous improvements and modifications occurred, resulting in the eventual emergence of the "Small Box" respirator in the later months of 1916.

Little other individual protective equipment emerged during the Great War, beyond impregnated leather gloves and linseed oil impregnated suits for occasional use by troops in areas where mustard gas had been employed. These items were not in general use however and the war ended before the particular problems associated with protection of the skin against mustard had been studied. The only other notable protective equipment to emerge was a cover for messenger pigeon baskets. Some desultory studies on the use of fans designed by a Mrs Hertha Ayrton, widow of a distinguished electrical engineer, to disperse gas from trenches were soon abandoned. The respirators were generally made by a large group of anti-gas factories in London and Nottingham set up through the Contracts Branch of the War Office. The numbers produced were vast e.g. 13,500,000 "Small Box" respirators and 14,000,000 Phenate Hexamine helmets: each "Small Box" respirator had 105 individual components. At Porton, from 1917 the Anti-Gas Department was primarily concerned with the collective protection of troops in dugouts and trenches by means of blanket curtains, and evaluation of British and foreign respirators in the field under realistic conditions, especially the vulnerability of the German respirator to British gases. Several distinguished scientists and medical men were associated with the Anti-Gas Department in London and later at Porton, notably Major (later Professor) E H Starling and Lieutenant Colonel C Lovatt Evans (later Professor Sir Charles Lovatt Evans FRS; who returned to Porton at the start of the Second World War and again after his retirement in the 1950s). Another pioneer of early respirators was Lieutenant (later Major) J A Sadd OBE who subsequently held senior civilian appointments at Porton until the early 1950s. Others of the Great War who subsequently served for many years at Porton in either military or civilian capacities and who can still be recalled by a few retired staff included Lieutenant Colonel W A Salt, Lieutenant Colonel A E Kent, Captain S J Steadman (at both CDES and MRD) and Lieutenant A C Peacock.

Crossley describes and illustrates the accommodation for troops at the Station; these were in the conventional military "lines", eight rows of eight huts each accommodating 15 men. Other huts were provided for photographers, meteorology, the Medical Officer and the Medical Inspection room, the Labour Company Office, Sergeants' Messes and accommodation, the offices of the Experimental Battery Royal Artillery and the Experimental Company Royal Engineers, the Commandant, the Royal Army Service Corps unit, dining halls, kitchens, concert hall, fire brigade, recreation rooms, supper bar, canteen and bath houses. The Station generated its own electricity from a power house, backed by accumulators for lighting at night. Extensive machine and carpenters' shops, foundries and blacksmiths' shops existed, not only to sustain the self-sufficiency of the Station in repairs but in alterations and adaptations to shells and weapons and the construction of laboratory and field equipment. A magazine was originally set up in an old barn but towards the end of 1916, the increase in artillery trials led to the construction of a purpose-designed magazine on the site of the latter-day Officers' Mess. This was linked to the ranges by the light railway. In 1917 another magazine was set up at Porton South but by 1918 the number of shell in the main magazine, in proximity to the main array of huts, was causing some concern. Eventually after the war, a new magazine was built in a more isolated position on the range, where the present complex of Range and magazine buildings are located.

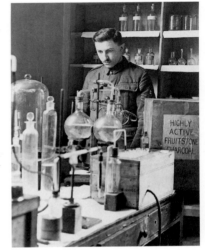

In the hutted laboratories at Porton Down during the Great War.

The Porton Mess

The Porton Mess existed from 1916 to 1979 having occupied several buildings during its sixty-three years. During the Great War it was set up in the Manor House at Idmiston, originally occupied by Lord Normanton. After the war, the house was condemned as insanitary and the Mess moved to the present Main Block or Headquarters building and adjacent huts and tents. Such inadequacies resulted in the completion of a new Mess in 1924.

The Mess was unusual in that after the Great War, the majority of its members were not Service Officers but civilian staff. Such staff were admitted according to their grade and for decades membership was limited to those of the Scientific Officer class and

Chief and Senior grades of the Experimental Officer class. In 1969 membership was extended to all grades of the latter class when the recommendations of the Fulton report on the Scientific Civil Services was implemented and again in 1971 when a further extension occurred. At the time of its closure, the Mess was open to a wide range of non-industrial staff. Perhaps the major value of the mess was the way in which it perpetuated the concept of the Porton tradition. It also enabled a variety of ages and grades from both the major Porton Establishments to get to know each other on a social basis that might not otherwise have been possible. Kent, in his 1960 "History of Porton" described it as "a focal point of Porton" and believed that "there is no other similar institution in any establishment in the country that has contributed so much to the work". He also suggests that an appreciation of this fact was evinced when the Canadian Experimental Station, Suffield was set up. Its Chief Superintendent insisted on the Mess in the Canadian Station being set up on the same lines: he too was convinced that Porton's success was "due to a significant extent to the unique character of the Officers Mess". The Porton Mess was the scene for Quarterly Dinners, Ladies Nights, Christmas and New Year events and notably the Annual Cocktail Party. Distinguished and less distinguished visitors and guests were entertained in the mess and it also provided accommodation, lunches and memorable dinners for the several Boards and Committees which advised both Establishments. The Mess also provided quarters for Service officers and civilian members; the latter gradually becoming predominant, especially when the Army largely departed from Porton in 1957.

Part of the top table at the Porton Down Officers Mess on 9 February 1979 at the dinner to mark the closure of the Mess. Left to right the figures are Dr R J C Harris, Director of the Microbiological Research Establishment and President of the Mess; Lieutenant Colonel T A K Watson, The Blues and Royals and President of the Mess Committee; Dr R G H Watson, Director of the Chemical Defence Establishment; Mr Eric Haddon, Director of the Chemical Defence Experimental Establishment from 1961–1968 and Wing Commander E D Blake, Air Force Experimental Officer and Secretary of the Mess.

Sketches by Fred May circa 1936. Where this was originally published is not known.

A most important unit of the British Army is the CHEMICAL DEFENCE EXPERIMENTAL STATION, whose na... explains its duties. These sketches were made by Fred May at a recent farewell dinner at H.Q., Port... Salisbury Plain, to Colonel J. U. Hope on his retirement, after thirty-six years in the Service; and his c... temporary, Major-General Lewis, who is being relieved by General Clarke. The C.D.E.S. was formed in 19... under the Ministry of Munitions as a school for the investigation of chemical warfare. In 1920 it w... reorganised, as the Chemical Defence Research Station.

The final dinner for one hundred and eleven members to mark the closure of the Mess was held on the 9th of February 1979. The former Mess now houses the Conservation Museum and the telephone exchange but most is devoted to the Sector's new Science Park which provides accommodation and amenities for civil firms.

For many members the loss of the Mess was as dismal and unnecessary an event as the closure of MRE. CAMR could not provide financial subsidies and essentially the Director of CDE chose to save money by closing the Mess. In later years a move to resurrect the Mess failed; this important Porton facility was lost for ever.

The Range

In 1999 the range at Porton is a sanctuary for some 96 species of birds, almost 200 species of spiders, and innumerable varieties of fungi, orchids and lichens; the area has been designated a Site of Special Scientific Interest. A prime reason for the exceptional flora and fauna is that the chalk grassland is relatively undisturbed and untouched by pesticides, fertilisers and the plough. Whilst sheep graze parts of the range, in other areas the turf is grazed by a vast rabbit population. The short turf provides optimum conditions for the now rare stone curlew. Scrub, and notably Juniper bushes, is slowly invading the grassland where sheep grazed for centuries before the Army came to Porton. This scrub in turn provides a habitat for many nesting birds. Over 100 deer and badgers exist on the range. The wooded areas are carefully managed with conservation interests in mind. Studies on Porton's natural history have

The Porton Ranges.
In July 1992 English Nature and CBDE signed a Management Plan for the Site of Special Scientific Interest which constitutes about half of the 7,000 acres of Ranges at Porton. This Management Plan will help to ensure the maintenance and enhancement of the outstanding features of the site.

been pursued for some years by an active Conservation Group, which also hosts visits from other interested and involved groups and bodies.

But the range is not only a vast 7000 acre nature reserve: it is an important archaeological area where so far more than 200 sites have been recorded. Some have been excavated but most remain untouched. There are 115 round barrows of the Bronze Age including the largest bell barrow in Wiltshire and 32 km of earthworks. Man has lived at Porton since early prehistory and his relics survive in barrows, cemeteries, earthworks, flint mines and enclosures. The flint mines at two separate sites of over 100 shafts each are important examples of Neolithic industry. The archaeological sites have been protected for decades, unlike the situation elsewhere, where the loss of sites to agriculture, to industry and land development, has been disastrous. In fact, most of the range has never been cultivated and can readily be described as a prehistoric landscape.

The state of the Porton range in 2000 emphasises the care taken to preserve defence lands. It also suggests that the environmental effect of disseminating chemical agents on the range in the considerable quantities that occurred notably between 1916 and the late 1950s has had little or no deleterious effect on the local flora and fauna. The ownership of the range by the Ministry of Defence and DERA has been a major factor in ensuring the preservation of a considerable heritage of natural history and archaeology.

Conservation at Porton Down

In common with other DERA and MOD sites, the CBD Sector is highly conscious of its responsibilities in conservation, especially in the fields of nature and archaeology. A little under a half of the Porton Range area was designated a Site of Special Scientific Interest in 1992 and a management plan was drawn up with English Nature. This enabled the CBD Sector to continue effective use of the Range in a manner compatible with defence needs whilst protecting and enhancing the unique environment of the area. From 1971–1979 the Bustard Trust made unsuccessful attempts to breed the Great Bustard in a range compound.

In 1992 the Range was declared a Special Protection Area under the European Commission Directive on the Conservation of Wild Birds. In 1996 the Sector won the Silver Otter Award for its work with the stone curlew. In 1997 the Royal Society for the Protection of Birds recorded twenty-one pairs of this rare species on the Range, representing about twelve per cent of the British

Battery Hill, earlier known as Spion Kop, with the gun sheds in the centre and the then MRE's water reservoirs in the foreground.

One of the larger tumuli on the Porton Range. The Battery Hill gun shed is just discernible on the right hand skyline.

population and the largest concentration in England. Between 1944 and 1997 a total of forty-four butterfly species were recorded, making Porton Range one of the premier butterfly sites in Great Britain and possibly the richest. Mycological studies have recorded over four hundred fungi, including seventy species which are nationally rare. As part of the Range is the largest tract of undisturbed chalk grassland in Great Britain, the Range supports a vast array of botanical species, including fifteen orchids. Macro-moth species collected amount to nearly three hundred.

Most of the Porton Range has never been ploughed, except for a small area which was steam-ploughed in the 19th Century. This has been providential for the archaeology of the site. Archaeology at Porton probably started in the late 1920s and the 1930s with Dr J F Stone (1899–1957) whilst a member of the then Chemical Defence Experimental Station. Later, during the Second World War, Stone became a senior member of the staff of Biology Department, Porton, and eventually of the Microbiological Research Establishment at Porton. Stone was originally a chemist and an enthusiastic and eminent amateur archaeologist, author of a book on archaeology in Wessex and many papers in archaeological journals.

At the time of the Armistice, manpower at Porton was 916 officers and other ranks, 33 women of The Queen Mary's Army Auxiliary Corps, about 500 civilian workmen and the sole civilian scientist, Mr Joseph Barcroft. The women acted as typists and shorthand writers: an old photograph shows them posed formally outside their quarter in "The Grange" at Hairpin Bend, This Corps (originally the Women's Army Auxiliary Corps) was disbanded in 1918. It was the forerunner of the Auxiliary Territorial Service and the Women's Royal Army Corps of the Second World War and after.

Hardly any vestiges now remain of the Station as it was in the Great War, beyond one of the stores buildings and the present headquarters building, designed by B F G Wakefield, who served at Porton from 1917–1919 as "Resident Architect" whilst with the Ministry of Munitions. This was under construction at the time of the Armistice and is now a Grade II Listed Building. Contemporary photographs show that most of the building work was done by soldiers of the Royal Engineers. The hutted "lines" of the Great War remained for some years until new barrack blocks were built. Despite the vast numbers of civilian workmen, the military nature of the Station in the Great War is quite evident and indeed this continued for many years until the Army largely withdrew in the 1950s.

The discharge of gases from cylinders, first emplaced and

Autumn at Old Lodge.
One of the old drives near the plantations in the Old Lodge area of the Porton Range.

Ladies of the Queen Mary's Army Auxillary Corps outside their quarters in a house on the edge of the village of Idmiston during the Great War. Their shoulder-flash carries the earlier initials WAAC.

then mounted in railway trucks or lorries, preoccupied the British for an untoward period. Grave shortages in the munition industry produced added problems and the United Kingdom was slow to follow German interest in the alternative means of delivering gas on-target by shells. Eventually we developed the Livens projector, a crude trench mortar, fired in batteries so that "crash shoots" of several thousand projectiles or Livens "drums" could produce an instantaneous and massive concentration of gas in the enemy lines. Firing trials with the Livens projector occupied an increasing part of activity at Porton, as did eventually the firing of shells. Particular technical problems were maximising efficiency of gas dissemination from the bursting munition, design of fuzes, minimising the decomposition of gas by the explosive forces, and the effect of ground temperature, wind and other parameters on the travel of the gas cloud formed from the burst of the munition.

The first meteorologist at Porton was Corporal T A Beardsmore BSc RE who occupied a small hut on the site in 1916 and was notionally commanded by a Colonel H G Lyons from some unit on Salisbury Plain. Up to 1920 no effort had been made to recruit civilian meteorologists for Porton due to the uncertainty of its future meteorological programme. By 1921 N K Johnson, later Sir Nelson Johnson, had been appointed the Superintendent of the new Meteorological Department, with the role of research on meteorological problems arising in chemical warfare and the use of smoke, and to provide a forecasting service for the Station. By 1925, three more meteorologists had been recruited and a wide range of research topics were being explored. In 1929, O G Sutton, later Sir Oliver Graham Sutton, joined the group and launched new work on dispersion which lasted into the 1930s. Sutton's work subsequently dominated thinking on dispersion for many years. Frank Pasquill joined in 1937 to study dispersion over the sea. After war service on trials in Australia he returned to Porton and

The Royal Engineers building the Headquarters Building in July 1918.

started a major study of long-range dispersion. Pasquill's work on wind borne material provided concepts still used by the international meteorological world. Meteorology continued on a one man basis at Porton until the late 1980s, albeit that the Meteorology Division had been dissolved some years earlier because of the Meteorological Office decision to centre its research at Bracknell and because of the declining number of field trials at Porton. Notwithstanding, several onetime Porton meteorologists became Director General of the Meteorological Office and achieved Fellowships of the Royal Society. Meteorological research was an important field at Porton, which contributed greatly to the understanding of how the weather influences gases and microscopic particles dispersed into the atmosphere.

More problems arose from the German use of shells charged with mustard gas in June 1917. The extraordinary vesicancy of this gas in both vapour and liquid form, its persistency on terrain and equipment and the effects on the eyes made this of great significance. Although not quick acting like chlorine or phosgene, mustard was relatively odourless and insidious. Casualty levels could not be limited by protecting the eyes and respiratory tract alone with a gas mask, since both vapour and liquid droplets exerted effects through the skin. The Station began a study of persistency, decontamination of man, equipment, houses and terrain. Bleach powder or paste was found to be a relatively simple decontaminant. However, it was evident that certain grave problems of protecting the feet, hands and body without serious physiological penalties and detriment of military efficiency, had to be solved. The war ended before these topics were addressed fully, although proofed leather gloves and boots had been evaluated. The development of defence against mustard gas was left for the inter-war years, as was the development of chemical warfare from the air and the study of its attendant problems.

The Armistice was celebrated with some enthusiasm by the troops at Porton; according to an autobiographical fragment by Sir Austen Anderson those in charge of the animals released a considerable number of monkeys; these reportedly frightened the occasional farm worker in the district over the ensuing weeks before eventually disappearing from sight. In recognition of Porton's role, King George V visited the Station on 16 September 1918. A few faded photographs remain to commemorate this visit. Crossley records that the Monarch "observed some experiments". Reputedly he was also amused by the chance discovery of a cake baking in a laboratory oven. Regrettably, the few known photographs of the visit are very poor, whereas most of the photographs of

The Livens projector.
The simple mortar displayed in this instructional photograph, was emplaced in batteries and fired electrically to deliver a "crash shoot" of bombs filled with phosgene, usually with devastating effect to a range of 1300–2000 metres. Nevertheless it was essentially a static weapon and laborious to deploy. Curiously, it persisted as an in-service weapon until the early days of the Second World War.

the Great War years at Porton are of superb quality. Possibly the photographer, overcome by the grandeur of the occasion, had failed to estimate the correct exposure or hold the camera steady.

Major General C H Foulkes, who had commanded the Royal Engineers Special Brigade during the war, resented what he saw as an inadequate post war acknowledgement by officialdom of the role and value of British gas warfare. He decided to write his own account and published his "Gas! The story of the special brigade" in 1934. Buckingham Palace refused permission for the inclusion of photographs of King George and Queen Mary visiting chemical warfare related sites in France or, indeed, any association of the royal family with gas warfare. Field Marshall Lord Cavan wrote that "I foresee hostile criticism if their Majesties are associated with gas development whether defensive, retaliatory or protective". This attitude was first identified by Professor Donald Richter in his 1992 book. The establishments at Porton Down were treated to a quick visit by the Duke of Edinburgh on 27 May 1956. This and the 1918 visit by King George V have been the only royal visits.

The early years of the Station were pioneering in the acquisition of entirely new knowledge despite the exigencies of war and the inability to approach the matter systematically. There were clearly frustrations, particularly from the complexity of other departments beyond Porton concerned with chemical warfare (these have not all been mentioned much here but were essentially the Special Brigade Royal Engineers and the artillery on the

The visit of King George V on 16 September 1918. The King is escorted by Crossley.

Western front i.e. the users, the chemical industry, the munition industry, the Trench Warfare Department and the Royal Army Medical Corps). However, the Great War saw Porton lay down the principles for the study of chemical warfare and chemical defence, using the integration of the multi-disciplinary approach and evaluation under realistic field conditions. It also saw the accumulation of a unique database and the establishment of a permanent military facility at Porton. Indeed, until very recent times most local people used the term "Porton Camp" to identify all or any of the distinct Establishments at Porton. The "Silver Star" buses which served the Establishment and village needs for decades always carried the destination of "Porton Camp" and there is still at least one finger post in the vicinity (at the cross-roads in Porton village) which carries this legend.

Assessment of the impact of the use of gas in the Great War on the Western, Eastern, and Italian fronts is difficult. Analysis of casualty figures is doomed to failure, because of a contemporary lack of definition and classification. Gas casualty estimates by several national official sources exceed a million but elements of uncertainty exist on the precise cause of death or major source of injury in those who were both gassed and wounded. Also, comparison of gas and other battlefield injuries shows vast swings in the proportions on different fronts in different years. Latter-day studies by L F Haber described in his 1986 book "The Poisonous Cloud: Chemical Warfare in the First World War" suggest that data on casualties, the cost of chemical munitions and their use, and attempts at a cost-effective analysis, lead to a dead end. The story of gas in the Great War on all sides is one of experiment and imitation conducted on a background of uncertainty and hurriedly assembled arrangements for both development, production and use. This was compounded by unfamiliarity and a lack of confidence, both to exploit gas warfare to the fullest and to seize the initiatives revealed after successful attacks. Further, some methods of use were patently crude. The real utility of gas in the Great War cannot be determined. It brought no great victories yet it had an obvious military impact. Those who remained unprotected were vulnerable' to the extent that all armies perceived the need to have high levels of gas protection and, where possible, to develop and maintain the ability to retaliate-in-kind. The advent of mustard gas emphasised such needs. The greater impact was perhaps to evoke a level of public horror subsequently reflected in political concern of a magnitude sufficient to press for the very legality of gas warfare to be considered and for arms control measures to be applied. A major factor influencing both public and official minds was the apparent

Mobile gas attack: a 1932 reconstruction.
Whilst the earliest use of cylinders was based on fixed installations, in the later stages of the Great War the "Beam Attack" was developed. Here the cylinders, deployed in lorries or railway trucks were opened simultaneously to provide a continuous, cone-shaped "beam" of gas which could penetrate, over a narrow front, deep into enemy territory.

A NCO of the Royal Engineers in the magazine compound at Porton during the Great War. He stands next to a 1650 lb "SN" bomb, which were the largest such munitions of the period and known as "bloddy paralysers". There is no evidence of the charging of such bombs with chemical agent, though aircraft bombing trials were planned at Porton in 1918 and at the time of the Armistice it was intended to conduct trials with larger bombs.

future vulnerability of the civil population to the use of aerial gas bombs in war.

In the Services, there were conflicting views on the matter of chemical weapons. Some senior officers were for the urgent development of gas warfare as an essential in future wars: others were less convinced, although conscious of the possible penalties of non-possession. Some thought that problems of defence were so great that no consideration should be given to any use of gas in future wars. This view probably arose because of fears that military scientists might de-stabilise conventional military doctrine to the extent that the conventional means of war familiar to the professional soldier would be subsumed in the still unconventional gas warfare. Equally, those with personal experience of gas in the trenches had other and humanitarian reasons for setting their faces against the further development of these means of war. Emotive assessments were undoubtedly made. The enthusiasts for the chemical arm pressed the alternative humanitarian view that short-term incapacitation from chemicals was the rule, rather than death and that, apart from the deaths associated with the early cloud attacks against unprotected or poorly protected troops, gas warfare had not resulted in a large proportion of casualty deaths. J B S Haldane in a now rare 1925 book "Callinicus: a defence of chemical warfare" states "that of the 150,000 British mustard gas casualties less than 4,000 (1 in 200) became permanently unfit". (He also describes in this little volume how "someone placed a drop of the liquid on the chair of the Director of the British Chemical Warfare Department. He ate his meals off the mantelpiece for a month"). Meanwhile, at Porton a sense of anti-climax prevailed.

The Old Portonians

The term "Old Portonians" has, of course, been used informally to describe in generic terms any former member of what is now the CBD Sector, or in a slightly different sense, any older and long serving member of the present staff. However, in 1992 papers came to light which revealed that the term "Old Portonians" was first used specifically for the Service officers who were at Porton Down during the Great War under Lieutenant Colonel Arthur Crossley, the first Colonel Commandant. In 1992 the then CBDE was presented by Mr T R Hall of Yatesbury in Wiltshire with a 15 carat gold lucifer or vestas match case presented to his late father Lieutenant S R Hall by Crossley and bearing the inscription "SHR 1917–19 Porton" on one side, and on the other "from AC". There was also a battered attaché case containing the records of the "Old

Portonians" which provided the first intimations that in 1919, Crossley's officers had formed a group entitled the "Old Portonians" to perpetuate their wartime comradeship and devotion to Porton Down, and their devotion to their Colonel Commandant. This group existed from 1919 to the outbreak of the Second World War. Samuel Hall was "Officer i/c Transport" at Porton during the Great War and eventually the Secretary of the group in 1939. Essentially, the group members kept in touch by newsletter and a yearly dinner at the Trocadero Restaurant at Piccadilly Circus. Correspondence attests to the anguish of the "Old Portonians" when Crossley died on 5 March 1927. A memorial tablet to Crossley, originally intended by the "Old Portonians" for Idmiston Church, (the scene of the Colonel's last church parade) but eventually sited in the wooden hutted Garrison Church, was re-erected when the church was demolished in the late 1950s in the entrance hall of the Headquarters building at Porton Down, where it still remains. It is doubtful if any of these original "Old Portonians" are still alive. Some became notable; at least three became knighted and three became Fellows of the Royal Society. What is remarkable is the way in which they attempted to perpetuate that now almost unfathomable ésprit-de-corps established at Porton under Crossley during the Great War. The gold match case and the silver cigar and cigarette box presented in 1924 to the "Officers of the Experimental Station, Porton, by the Officers of the original Establishment", and inscribed with their names, remains on display with other Porton Mess silver in the Main Conference Room of the Headquarters building.

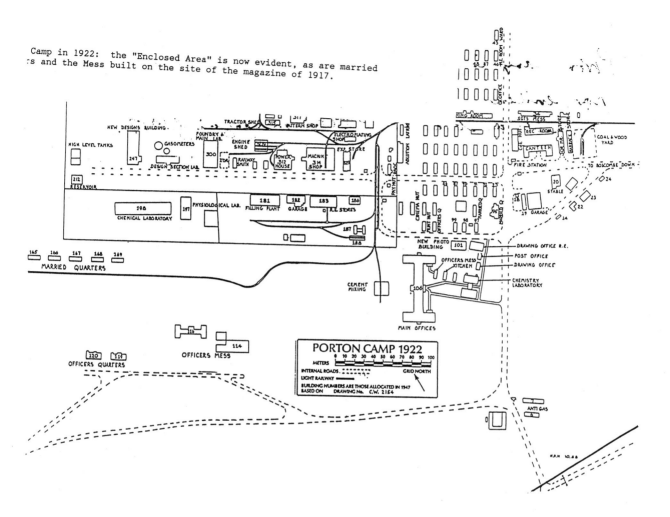

Camp in 1922: the "Enclosed Area" is now evident, as are married
:s and the Mess built on the site of the magazine of 1917.

The Inter-War Years 1919–1939

2

Uncertainty, Consolidation and More Uncertainty

At the Armistice, Porton was controlled by the Chemical Warfare Department, set up in 1917 with its headquarters in London, supporting the Chemical Warfare Committee and the Chemical Designs Committee (concerned with offensive equipment and munitions) and in addition to Porton, an anti-gas section at University College London, a research and small-scale experimental station at Wembley, and small units within many universities and scientific institutes. At Porton a massive exodus occurred. Soon, Service personnel numbers were reduced to skeleton levels and activity quickly expired in the face of lack of staff and uncertainty about the future role of the Station. Eventually, it was decided to shut down all parts of the Department except the London headquarters and Porton. The Chemical Warfare Department was transferred from the Ministry of Munitions to the War Office on 1 July 1919 where it became subordinate to the Director of Artillery under the Master General of the Ordnance, where it remained until 1939. Crossley spent some early part of 1919 writing the "Crossley Report" but made no recommendations therein as to the future course of research, nor indeed did he refer at all to the future of Porton or of gas warfare.

In May 1919 a committee under the chairmanship of Lieutenant General Sir Arthur Holland was set up to investigate and report on the organisation of chemical warfare and to make recommendations on the needs of peacetime research at Porton. Its report was to chart the next 20 years: one practical import was the end of separate offensive and defensive research and development. The Cabinet agreed the suggestions from the committee and decided that research was to continue at Porton pending any decision by the League of Nations on the legitimacy of chemical warfare and on disarmament, and the subsequent level of United Kingdom accord with the international consensus. This decision, in 1920, led to a slow programme of new building at Porton, the reconstitution of the Chemical Warfare Committee and the gradual recruitment of civilian scientists. Married quarters, officers' and NCOs messes, barracks, a Commandant's residence, laboratories, workshops, gas chambers and experimental munition filling plant were built during the 1920s. What has for years been termed the

Porton Camp in 1922: the "Enclosed Area" is now evident, as are married quarters and the Mess built on the site of the magazine of 1917.

"Closed Area", to the immediate north-west of the headquarters building became the new focus for most of the scientific and technical buildings. The married quarters formed a parallel area outside the enclosing fence whilst the barracks were sited to the north-east. Throughout the 1920s most of the hutted lines of the Great War disappeared. The buildings at the Establishment are of interest, though largely utilitarian. Amazingly there were over 400 in the early 1990s; they vary from the elegant colonial facaded headquarters building to utilitarian brick boxes. Some have a certain quality or even charm. The 1937 building currently housing parts of the Medical and Biology Division is of that military architectural style of the period, sometimes called "Hore-Belisha", after the one-time Secretary of State for War. The 1922 chemistry laboratory building, demolished in 1991 was plain and industrial with tall rooms and herring-bone roof windows resembling those of factories of the period. Perhaps most intriguing is that built in 1927-28 as the Offensive Munitions Section. This briefly held title was soon changed to Technical Chemistry Section. The building, with its grey walled cloisters surrounding a central lawn has more than a faint monastic appearance. With the advent of modern new buildings in 1999, many of the old buildings are due for demolition. The engineering and other workshops of the Station reflected its manifold needs, the geographical isolation and the urge to attain self-sufficiency. In the Great War, many soldiers had manned the workshops; later the main engineering workshops were largely staffed by naval ratings, both artificers and seamen together with officers from the Corps of Naval Constructors and an Engineer Lieutenant Commander.

The Engineering Section

The Section was initially a Porton branch of the Portsmouth Dockyard workshops and was seen as a Naval Shore Station, with

The scientific and executive staff at Porton in November 1928: the Director of Experiments, Mr N K Johnson, is sitting next to the Commandant and Lieutenant Colonel A E Kent, the author of an earlier history of Porton is seated sixth from the left. Several other veterans of the Royal Engineers Special Brigade appear in this photograph.

about forty ratings under the command of a Commander (E). In April 1922 the ratings were "civilianised" but the officers remained on the active list. The unit was housed in two corrugated iron hangars, known as South Workshops. After the hangars were condemned as unsafe in 1930, negotiations started to have them replaced by brick buildings.

Between 1920 and 1924 the South Workshops came under the control of the Superintendent of the Defensive Munitions Department and began increasingly to produce the Service's Mark III and Mark IV respirators because of the difficulty in getting such work done by industry. By 1924 another workshop was started under the aegis of the Technical Chemistry Department in what was known as the Old Foundry. This concentrated on the making of prototype chemical weapons. In 1928 when the Technical Chemistry Division moved to new buildings, the workshop went with it. However, by 1937 the staff and machinery moved into other buildings belonging to the Defensive Munitions Department and known as the Lay-apart Store. This soon became the North Workshop. By 1939 it had been decided that the workshops should be combined under a new department, called firstly the Design and Production Department and by 1942, the Engineering Section. From 1930s continuous efforts were made to get a new workshop building to replace the condemned South Workshop. By 1939 financial approval was obtained but construction was negated on the grounds that it might be unwise to construct major new buildings during the war. After the end of the war, efforts were renewed. Eventually, building of the present workshops began in 1948. Three bays were finished by 1949 and some sections of the Engineering Section moved in, leaving the remainder of the Section scattered about the site. Eventually, work on completion started in 1953 and was finished by 1954. The new Engineering Section workshops were inspired by Sir Henry Tizard, the Chairman of both the Advisory Council for Scientific Policy and the Defence Research Policy Committee who suggested to the Chief Superintendent shortly after the end of WWII that Porton should be rebuilt on a carefully thought out site plan, taking advantage in the grouping of buildings to improve the efficiency of the Station as a whole. To a degree the Bateman Plan of 1947 (see page 72) was a product of Tizard's vision. The completion of the new Engineering Section was seen as a major part of Edgar Bateman's planning within CDES. Regrettably, defence economies held up the Bateman implementation. Tizard's visions were known, somewhat mockingly, to senior staff as the "Brighter Porton" scheme; they clearly saw substantial architectural improvements as unlikely. For these, Porton would have to wait until the end of the 20th century.

The facilities available in the Engineering Section were impressively comprehensive and of the highest quality, backed by a large drawing office and a staff of design engineers. Its capabilities included instrument making, foundry work, milling, turning, shaping, sheet metal working and welding. There was a sailmakers shop, joinery and a materials group capable of producing almost any moulding in plastic and rubber formulation. The Establishment ceased in the 1970s, like all other MOD establishments, to be involved in development work. This was contracted out to industry. Inevitably, the number of Engineering Section staff fell dramatically from a staff of 170 to about 30. The apprentice scheme was also abandoned.

Staffing remained something of a Station problem in the 1920s. Civilian scientists appointments were temporary and an element of uncertainty about the future prevailed In 1922 there were 380 officers and men of the Services at Porton but a mere 23 civilian scientific and technical officers and 25 "civilian subordinates". By 1925 the number of civilian staff had doubled. Many staff of the early 1920s had belonged to the short-lived body called "The Chemical Roster", which appeared to be both newly recruited men or the residues of long-service Special Brigade Royal Engineer men, grouped on similar lines to armament artificers elsewhere, as a branch of the Royal Engineers, administered by the Experimental Company Royal Engineers (later the 58th (Porton) Company RE). The "Chemical Roster" was disbanded soon after 1922 and many men were re-employed as civilians.

The Holland Committee report had stressed the need for fundamental research and stressed that this was dependent on attracting scientists of the right type "Nothing short of £2000 a year could be relied upon to induce a man of the first rank to accept the post of Director of Research at Porton". The general programme of research and development required was laid down in 1920 by the Services and the Chemical Warfare Committee. The main areas were individual respiratory protection, the collective protection of HM ships, the design of more efficient weapons and munitions especially aerial gas bombs, the meteorology of gas and smoke clouds and the treatment of gas casualties. The annual reports from 1921–1938, which were published successively by the Chemical Warfare Committee, the Chemical Warfare Research

---

[5] Originally "HM Factory, Sutton Oak", then "The Research Establishment, Sutton Oak", and later the "Chemical Defence Research Establishment Sutton Oak", this was the Department's process research plant for agent-production studies until 1952. It was at St Helens in Lancashire and was resited at Nancekuke in Cornwall from 1952 until its closure in 1979.

Department and (from 1930) the Chemical Defence Research Department, provide a detailed account of the progress of the programme at Porton, Sutton Oak[5] and in extramural studies. They also provide the definitive account of United Kingdom policy, doctrine and planning up to the Second World War. (These reports are in the Public Record Office, in "0 and A" papers W033). The reports lack great detail on all but the military and most senior civilian staff and personalities at Porton. They do however provide meticulous details of the membership of the Chemical Warfare Committee and the subsequent Chemical Defence Committee, their associate members and sub-committees. The outstanding impression from such lists is the great eminence of those associated with the Department and Porton in the inter-war years. Household names in the world of science and medicine abound: Professor F A Lindemann (later Lord Cherwell, Churchill's personal scientific adviser during World War II), Professor R A Peters (later Sir Rudolph Peters); H H Dale (later Sir Henry Dale) Lord Rayleigh; Lord Rutherford; Lovatt Evans; Joseph Barcroft; J S Haldane; Sir Harold Hartley; Sir William Bragg; Professor Perkin; Professor AM Tyndall and many others. Regrettably, none of these reports have descriptions of the fabric of the Station, nor of the way in which day-to-day activity was pursued. In fact, there seems to be no readily accessible means of picturing life at Porton in the 1920s and 1930s. Anecdotes have been passed down the generations by word-of-mouth but memories of the inter-war years and of the Second World War, even amongst the oldest surviving retired members of staff have all but slipped away.

A Bombadier of the Royal Artillery in 1930, wearing the 1926 General Service respirator, with the Mark IV facepiece, as issued in 1927. The "GS" underwent several minor modifications until supplanted by the "Light Type Respirator" of 1942, which had the canister mounted on the facepiece, as does the modern S10 British respirator.

Prototype protection for army horses and mules 1938: a fragment of the Porton Light Railway is seen in the background.

A 1936 trial to determine the effect of a harrassing agent on the performance of a gun crew.

A 1938 trial at Tipnor Pond in Hampshire to determine the persistence of mustard gas on sand and shingle.

The unpublished "History of Porton" by Lieutenant Colonel A E Kent, who formerly served in the Special Brigade Royal Engineers in the Great War of 1914–1918, and later at Porton, both in uniform and as a civilian until 1954, is probably the major source of more parochial impressions. "Tony" Kent (1887–1972) was an intriguing character. Before the Great War he was a schoolmaster at Dunheved College in Launceston. He joined the army soon after the war started and by 1915 he was listed as a Lieutenant in the Special Reserve of Officers in the 3rd Battalion of the Leicestershire Regiment. In July 1915 he was seconded to one of the new Special Company's (later the Special Brigade of the Royal Engineers). Kent took part in the first British retaliatory gas attack at Loos on 25 September 1915. By 1918 he was an acting Lieutenant Colonel; he was awarded the MC in 1917 and the DSO in 1918. In November 1919, reverting to Captain, he was in command of the Experimental Company RE (formerly the Porton Detachment of "B" Company of the Special Brigade). By 1921 this was the 58th (Porton) Company RE. By 1924 Kent again held the rank of Lieutenant Colonel and remained in command until 1926. By 1938 Kent was Military Experimental Officer at Porton, responsible for the conduct of field trials. He continued in this post until 1948. On retirement from the Army he became a Senior Experimental Officer in the Trials Planning Section until finally retiring in 1954. Kent regarded himself as a Royal Engineer but never held an RE commission. He had always signed documents, using RE after his name but apparently was not entitled to do so, although the wearing of RE badges and buttons whilst serving with an RE unit was not unusual, since dress regulations were often ignored in special circumstances. Kent was saddened at retirement from the Army and apparently continued to wear his uniform at Porton for some considerable period after until remonstrated with by the Chief Superintendent and the Senior Military Officer. A considerable tribute was paid to this unique man in his obituary in "The Times" of 12 April 1972 by Sir Owen Wansbrough-Jones, formerly Chief Scientist of the Ministry of Supply. Kent, on his retirement in 1956, solicited a commission to write the history for £230. When it was finished in 1961 the then Director of CDEE, for reasons which are not now readily apparent, merely caused a summary booklet to be written based on Kent's text. This summary was prepared by C G Trotman when Head of the then Technical Information and Records Section and issued in 1961 as a booklet entitled "A brief history of the Chemical Defence Experimental Establishment, Porton". This Restricted document was available to an official readership. It was subsequently occasionally exposed to a wider public readership by successive Directors and eventually de-classified for unlimited access in 1987. As for Kent's large history, it was decided that it was equally unsuitable as an official history or, as Kent intended, a book for the general public. From 1962–1992 the typescript copies languished in the records of CDEE, where they nevertheless continued to be a largely unknown but nevertheless a major source of information. Kent's original introduction is worth paraphrasing: he writes that his history was aimed at a record of Porton's achievements, the process whereby civilians and servicemen had worked together, the national asset manifest in the unique facilities and expertise available not only for military purposes but for the civil sector, a record of Dominion and North American co-operation with the United Kingdom and finally to inspire "those now serving at Porton and to those who come after, and to bring a pride of achievement to many, including those now retired". The annual reports and "Kent's History" provide some occasional snippets of camp life, including the 1921 complement for officers, NCOs, men, civilians of several categories and horses. The Commander and Adjutant were each allotted two horses, the Lieutenant Colonel (Chief Technical Officer) one, the RA Battery 64 and the civilian Director of Experiments one. The holder of the latter appointment was also privileged to receive eight weeks leave a year, though lesser staff could attain this level when ten years service had been completed. In "Conditions of Employment for the Civilian Scientific Staff at the Experimental Station, Porton" it is intriguing to read that "private scientific work may be carried out by members of the staff in their spare time . . ." though "No private scientific work is to be published without permission, which will not be unreasonably withheld".

The 1929 Standing Orders for the Station give glimpses of military life but little of that of the civilian staff. We read of the

A 1938 trial to determine the droplet size of coloured simulants sprayed by aircraft on marching troops. Vertical and horizontal cards are carried by some soldiers who also have white sampling tippets on their shoulder.

specifications for poultry runs in married quarters, when fuel, oil, disinfectants, bread, meat and groceries could be drawn from the Barrack Services and Supplies, how "climbing onto hayricks or stacks for any purpose is strictly forbidden", conduct in the Officers' Mess, Post Office collection times, and the minutiae of military orders. Kent tends to relate minor events in ways reflecting a somewhat archaic sense of humour e.g. on the inadvertent aerial spraying of the married quarters with a dyed simulant and the discovery of a pink-spotted baby, Amesbury housewives dismayed by pink-spotted washing, the accidental destruction of a bursting chamber on the ranges, and japes during sea trials at Scapa Flow in 1923. Later, he is better with chapters on the "Porton Home Guard" and the "Officers' Mess: social and Recreational Activities" which included bits on the Porton Musical and Dramatic; Society and sports activities, notably the annual cricket matches between the Station and the chairmen of the many sub-committees of the Chemical Warfare Committee and the later Chemical Defence Board.

One of the major post-war tasks had been the assessment of the condition of a million wartime respirators. One per cent of the national stock was sent to Porton for penetration tests. The only convenient method was to do this by having men breathe through them whilst exposed to the irritant arsenical smoke DM (diphenyl-amine chloroarsine). These tests imposed some physical and physiological strain on the staff because the results were urgently needed and because the respirators were found to be largely

The Defensive Munitions Department, some time in the 1920s. The central foreground figure is Major J A Sadd, OBE, formerly of the Royal Engineers, the Superintendent of the Department and a pioneer in respirator design during the Great War. There are curious things in this photograph: note the spats worn by figure on the extreme right. Sadly, only about three of the group can be unequivocally recognised.

The Royal Artillery Detachment at the Royal Engineers Experimental Station in 1928.

penetrable and useless through deterioration. The deficiencies triggered Service requests for improved designs of respirators and the subsequent emergence of Naval and Army respirators and, by 1926, the common service OS respirator which became the standard pattern for the armed forces, until the "Light Type Respirator" of 1942 largely supplanted it. Some million OS respirators were produced before and during the Second World War, from the research and development of prototypes at Porton: all Commonwealth forces and much of the Air Raids Precautions (ARP) personnel were provided with this model.

Research into the protection of the hands, body and feet from mustard gas droplets and vapour during aerial attack was an important feature of the inter war years. During the Great War, the respirator alone had largely sufficed. Soldiers eventually learnt to

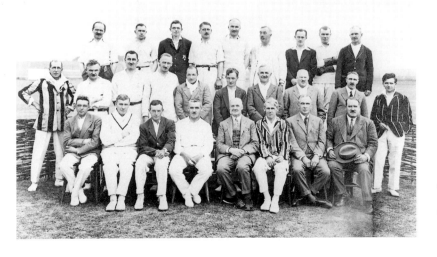

The Annual Cricket Match between the Station and the Chairmen of the Committees under the aegis of the Chemical Warfare Committee. The blazered figure in the front row is N K Johnson, the Director of Experiments at Porton: he was later, as Sir Nelson Johnson, Director of the Meteorological Office. The central suited figure is Professor (later Sir) Joseph Barcroft.

A Vickers Medium Mark II tank on the Porton Range in 1932 for trials on the vulnerability of tank crews to gas attack. This tank belonged to the 5th Battalion of the Royal Tank Corps. The "plus-fours" glimpsed on the right appeared to have been popular with senior scientific staff for wear on the Ranges.

A Fairey Albacore of the Fleet Air Arm engaged in trials over the Porton Ranges in the 1940s.

The aircraft is disseminating a dyed simulant for mustard gas from its SCI (Smoke Curtain Installation). The SCI could be used to disseminate smoke or chemical warfare agents and was one of the major British chemical weapons of the Second World War.

keep away from splashed liquid mustard gas. In those years there was no prospect of a more insidious exposure to small droplets of mustard gas sprayed from aircraft. Mustard vapour was effectively kept out of the eyes and respiratory tract by the respirator. However, as the air forces of the major nations developed and the feasibility of aerial bombing attacks on cities grew, ARP became an increasing national concern. The use of gas under such conditions posed enormous problems. In about 1926, the study of this topic was added to the responsibilities of the Station. As a result of Porton's work, at the outbreak of the Second World War the country was very well prepared and equipped, notably in the provision of a cheap but efficient civilian respirator together with children's and babies models, designed and developed at the Station for production by industry. Over 97 million of several types of civilian respirators were produced during the war. The United Kingdom was unique in providing such respirators, at no cost, to the whole of its population. (The actual cost to the Exchequer during the 1940s was about 15p in today's money for each respirator). It is significant that the first five ARP handbooks published from 1939 by the Home Office (but written at Porton) deal with protection against gas and the seventh deals with anti-gas precautions for merchant ships. Numerous other ARP memoranda and pamphlets were also largely written by anonymous Porton authors.

Aircraft and Porton

It is not clear when aircraft were first used for trials at Porton. It is possible that the 1919 British use of ad hoc chemical munitions based on thermogenerators to distribute particulate arsenicals against the Red Army in northern Russia was the first time that chemical warfare had been used from the air. These thermo-generator devices designed for smoke formulations had been fitted with fins and were literally hand-dropped from DH9 aircraft but there is no indication that any preliminary trials were done on the Porton Range. However, it is clear from the Crossley report of 1919 that there were trials with ad hoc bombs in progress at the time of the Armistice, albeit that their location was not stated. The newly founded Royal Air Force appeared to have had little contact with Porton at that time. There was a realisation that chemical agent dissemination by bombs or spray from aircraft was of considerable significance in the early years after the Great War, especially in the hazards which would be posed to civilian populations. However, offensive preparations by the Royal Air Force languished during the years of inter-war ambivalence about ethics, arms control and a reluctance to become committed to attacks against civil based industry. Thus, Porton remained the prime site for research on the most effective ways of using aerial chemical warfare and on how it could be defended against. In 1922 the first Air Force Experimental Officer (AFEO) was appointed at Porton, a post which was to continue until 1990, when the title became the Senior Air Force Officer or, occasionally, the Staff Officer (RAF).

In 1922 the AFEO was tasked to provide aircraft, as and when required, for Porton field trials, to deliver chemical warfare agents and smoke. The nearest aerodrome with suitable aircraft was RAF Netheravon which provided trials aircraft from a small unit entitled the Porton Experimental Flight. In 1931 this unit moved to the newly reopened RAF aerodrome at Boscombe Down, now DERA Boscombe Down and eventually was re-titled the Special Duty Flight. In 1946 the Flight was disbanded. Planes for Porton, for chemical, biological, smoke, pesticide and meteorological trials were then provided by B Flight of the then Aircraft and Armament Experimental Establishment, Boscombe Down. The use of aircraft, both rotary and fixed wing, for field trials of all sorts has diminished over the years. During the 1960s an RAF pilot was stationed at Porton to fly the aircraft held at Boscombe Down for Porton field trials. Inevitably, the use of aircraft in trials peaked during the Second World War. The first plane to be regularly used at Porton was probably an Avro 504K in 1928. No formal source of planes for Porton trial still exists at Boscombe Down. One of the last Hunter aircraft adopted for spraying simulants in field trials is now in the Boscombe Down museum. If planes were to be required at Porton in the future they would still be expected to come from Boscombe Down, now like the CBD Sector, a part of DERA.

Other products of Porton's research and development at the end of the 1930s include eye- shields to protect against high altitude liquid mustard gas attack (which would not be perceived and against which hazard the continuous battlefield wearing of the respirator would have been the impracticable alternative) the oilskin Cape Anti-Gas, impregnated battle dress (the treatment of fabrics with an "impregnite" capable of reacting with mustard gas was a considerable research topic before and during the Second World War), protective dubbin for boots, detectors and detector papers and paint (for gas on equipment and terrain), sleeve detectors (a paper tippet or sleeve worn on the shoulder or upper arm upon which agent droplets would produce a colour change), heaviest oilskin clothing for decontamination tasks, decontamination procedures and liquids, gas identification sets for service units, respirators and anti-gas covers for horses, mules and for war dogs Protection for camels was also studied; a prototype respirator exists still in the Sector.

There were probably no better equipped forces in respect of anti-gas defence than those of the United Kingdom in the late 1930s. We had emerged from the Great War of 1914–1918 with a respirator, techniques for gas-proofing dug-outs and buildings, and little else. At the end of the 1930s superior quality and scales of anti-gas equipment were available to the forces to cater for all known hazards. It is significant that during the Second World War the design of such equipment changed but little. Minor improvements were often incorporated from users experiences, or to reflect new threats. Occasionally during the Second World War inferior raw materials had to be utilised because of shortages usually these were speedily replaced after Porton research on alternatives.

In summary, in the inter-war years, the anti-gas defence of the United Kingdom and its forces had been brought to a level which was superior to that of any other nation. The basis of this lay in the research and field trials done at Porton. The development and production by industry were masterminded by the Chemical Defence Research Department under the aegis of the Master General of the Ordnance. However, as far as offensive capabilities were concerned investment had been limited and production had been minimal in terms of agents and weapons, due to pre-war political unease and uncertainties. This situation was to an extent redeemed by the small amount of relevant research and develop-

Two Hawker Audax and on the right a Hawker Hind at Porton in 1937. Aircraft for Porton trials were from the Special Duty Flight at Netheravon and later Boscombe Down. The title of the flight changed several times before 1946, when it was disbanded. Thereafter aircraft for Porton were operated on an ad hoc basis by "B" Squadron at Boscombe Down.

The interior of the onetime hutted Garrison Church at Porton Down pre-1957. Most of the memorial brasses seen on the right were re-erected in the Headquarters building at the time of the Establishment's 75th Anniversary.

ment which Porton and Sutton Oak had been permitted to pursue during the inter-war years on the ways in which chemical warfare might be used against the British and Imperial forces in any future war. By 1938 the international situation was such that offensive research and development and the production of war reserve stocks of mustard gas were authorised by the Cabinet, albeit that it was realised that a useful production output could not be obtained for 12 to 18 months and the retaliatory-use-only concept inherent in the United Kingdom's ratification of the Geneva Protocol remained. The Italian use of mustard gas against Abyssinia in 1936 was a harbinger of concerns which steadily increased in the United Kingdom, especially since Italy was a state party to the 1925 Geneva Protocol.

The Chemical Defence Research Establishment at Sutton Oak 1915–1954

The Chemical Defence Research Establishment (CDRE), Sutton Oak, St Helens, evolved from an old factory taken over by the Government in 1915. It had earlier been a copper works, a tube factory, a fertiliser factory, a glass works and steel works.

In 1915 UK Chemical Products Ltd re-opened it for the production of phenol and benzol. When the need for phenol diminished in 1917, it produced a limited amount of the arsenical chemical warfare agent diphenylchloroarsine, known as DA or Blue Cross and by the Germans as Blaukreuz. The factory was probably then closed until 1920, though still held by the Director General of Factories. In 1922 plant for making another arsenical chemical warfare agent diphenylamine chloroarsine was transferred from the HM Factory at Ellesmere Port. In 1925 the factory became a part of the London-based Chemical Warfare Research Department, the HQ of the United Kingdom chemical warfare and defence organisation. Its role was technical research for the ultimate transfer of laboratory scales of making agents to process plants for large scale production. Plants were available at Sutton Oak for diphenylamine chloroarsine and for mustard gas on a scale of a few tons per week. By 1944 it contained plants capable of production at scales of 4 cwts, 2 tons, 5 tons, 10 tons and 50 tons per week. It was not, however, a production factory: its essential role was the study and development of production processes. When a process was firmly established, details were passed to the chemical industry who could then proceed to full-scale production. Its unique experience in such development was occasionally used in different areas eg when the insecticide DDT was in short supply, Sutton Oak produced this on a 2 ton per week basis in 1944–1945. Munition filling or "charging" was also part of the programme in the 1930s. Charging machines of several sorts for aircraft bombs and Livens Drums were developed and the details passed to the Agency Factories in the 1930s. BAL (British Anti Lewisite) was also produced in the 1940s.

At the end of the Second World War, Sutton Oak's attention

The former Chemical Defence Research Establishment at Sutton Oak during the Second World War. This ancient place closed in 1953 and the site was sold in 1957.

was directed to the organophosphorus nerve agents which had been secretly developed and stockpiled by the Germans but were unknown to the Allies. A detailed study of the optimum production processes was made, starting with those which had been used by the Germans at Munsterlager for either the laboratory or pilot plant preparation of the nerve agents known as Tabun (GA), Sarin (GB), Soman (GD), Ethyl-Sarin (GE) and Cyclo-Sarin (GF). Sutton Oak also played the major part in the design of the bacterial pilot plant erected at Porton down for the Microbiological Research Department.

In 1947 it was decided that the CDRE site at Sutton Oak was too dangerous for development work with the highly toxic nerve agents at the pilot plant or full-scale plant level, because of the built-up areas within 250 metres and plans for further development within 150 metres: a more suitable and safer site would be sought. Ultimately, an airfield, formerly RAF Portreath, held on a care-and-maintenance basis at Nancekuke in Cornwall was selected. Nancekuke was taken over from the Air Ministry in 1949 and became the Chemical Defence Establishment, Nancekuke in 1951 and the move from Sutton Oak eventually began. Sutton Oak closed in 1953, the facilities were decontaminated and partially demolished and after sale in 1957 eventually became a site for light industry as the Reginald Road Industrial Estate.

The First Official Unease about Biological Warfare

It seems unlikely that any nation gave any serious thought to biological warfare until the 1920s. Before the latter half of the 19th Century one limiting factor was the lack of knowledge of the microbial origin of infectious diseases; though the concept of contagion was recognised earlier and many texts have cited archaic modes of biological warfare such as catapulting plague-ridden corpses into besieged cities in medieval times and distributing the bedding of smallpox victims to hostile North American Indians. In later years there was occasional speculation about the deliberate use of micro-organisms in war and in the Great War of 1914–1918 there were undoubtedly German attempts at infecting allied cavalry horses with glanders and anthrax. During the 1920s intelligence that other nations were beginning to take an interest in the potentials of biological warfare began to concern the Committee of Imperial Defence. The horror of gas which had arisen in the public mind during the Great War had combined with the urge for general disarmament to cause the League of Nations to negotiate the prohibition of gas warfare through the 1925 Geneva

Protocol. During negotiations in the early 1920s Poland suggested that the prohibition on the use of gas be extended to cover "bacteriological warfare" as "an arm discreditable to modern civilisation". The suggestion was readily accepted; although the subsequent states parties to the 1925 Geneva Protocol (often known as the Gas Protocol) can have had little real knowledge of the means whereby biological agents might be employed nor, indeed, any knowledge of feasibility beyond extrapolation from naturally occurring disease and medical microbiology.

Whilst the Geneva Protocol, which prohibited the use of chemical and biological agents in war, was a factor to be weighed in the minds of those who might otherwise have embarked in such use, it did imply to some that there might be military utility in such methods of war. Although there was an abhorrence of the concept, several nations recognised that they had to defend against it and some believed that possession of a retaliatory capability was a useful deterrence. Therefore, even though they eventually ratified the Protocol, several nations were stimulated into paying attention to biological warfare under conditions of great secrecy; as indeed they were quite entitled to do so, for the Protocol did not prohibit possession of the means of either types of warfare. Even the prohibition on use was virtually a no-first-use agreement. Nations like Japan and even America which, at that time had not ratified the Protocol, were under no obligation to even conform to its spirit. It is now certain that the former USSR began development of biological weapons as early as 1928. French and Japanese offensive research probably started in the same period.

Increasing intelligence during the 1930s about German interest in biological warfare led to the War Department seeking advice from Porton from the Medical Research Council and directors and deans of appropriate institutes and medical faculties such as Professor (later Sir John) J C G Ledingham, Director of the Lister Institute; Professor W W C Topley, Dean of the London School of Hygiene and Tropical Medicine and Dr S R Douglas, Director of the National Institute for Medical Research. Eventually, it was decided to formalise United Kingdom concern by the creation in 1936, of a Biological Warfare Sub-Committee of the Committee of Imperial Defence. The main influence behind this decision of the Minister for the Co-ordination of Defence was the Secretary of the Committee of Imperial Defence, Colonel Sir Maurice Hankey (later the first Lord Hankey) who remained a senior and controlling figure in the field for many years. The Sub-Committee, chaired by Hankey, included representatives from the medical services of the Royal Navy, the Army and the Royal Air

Force, the Home Office and the Medical Research Council, several senior scientists from outside the official areas and the Chief Superintendent of the Chemical Defence Research Department in London, Mr N K Johnson. Their mandate was to "report on the practicability of bacteriological warfare and to make recommendations as to the countermeasures which should be taken to deal with such an eventuality".

In the next four years the Sub-Committee prepared several major reports, mainly on defensive matters and notably on how vaccines could be made available. It was decided by the Committee of Imperial Defence in 1937 that the need for a capability for the United Kingdom to retaliate-in-kind need not be considered at present. A proposal to set up an Emergency Bacteriological Service was approved in 1938 by the Committee of Imperial Defence and the Sub-Committee was renamed the Committee of Imperial Defence Sub-Committee on Emergency Bacteriological Services, a move intended to reflect its defensive role. The name was then almost immediately changed; the existing title for the Service being thought "too disturbing to the public mind". At the suggestion of Sir Edward Mellanby the title became "The Emergency Public Health Laboratory Service" After the Second World War the word "emergency" was dropped and the Service continues today. The Service set up a number of laboratories, under the Ministry of Health but managed by the Medical Research Council; these became used for general public health work and still constitute the regional network of the Public Health Laboratory Service some laboratories being located within hospitals and others existing as separate entities. The Public Health Laboratory Service now has no biological defence role and its origins in such defence are mere matters of history.

Activity at Porton in the early months of 1939 clearly increased in intensity and pace. In August, the Establishment was transferred to the Ministry of Supply. The advent of war must have brought profound changes to everyday life at Porton, both for civilians and the military staff, yet there are virtually no comprehensive records available. The instructions and plans which inevitably must have been promulgated by the London headquarters and by the Commandant are no longer preserved at Porton. Some files of the period lie in the Public Record Office but clearly much of domestic and parochial interest disappeared long before such archives left the Departmental Records Office for the Public Record Office. Many orderly room files of interest were destroyed when the major military presence left Porton in 1957.

The Chemical Defence Experiment Station in 1940. The 1918 Headquarters are on the left. The barracks and the square in the foreground has Great War huts at each side.

THE SECOND WORLD WAR 1939–1945

3

The Prospect of Attack and Retaliation

There was a near-complete lack of chemical munitions at the onset of the war on 3 September 1939. No artillery munitions, Livens projector drums, mortar bombs, rockets or other devices charged with agent were stockpiled for Army use. A few 250 lb. mustard gas bombs for the RAF, together with some 250 lb spray tanks may have been available, since charging started in August and September 1939. Some 500 tons of mustard gas and 5 tons of tear gas were available in bulk stocks. Had the Germans initiated chemical warfare at the outbreak of war, the immediate ability of the United Kingdom to retaliate-in-kind would have been negligible. Retaliation-in-kind at this earliest stage of the war when the British Army had not engaged the German Army would have largely depended on the ability of the RAF to attack military and industrial targets in Germany. The nature of the British retaliation would have depended on what sort of targets in the United Kingdom had been attacked with chemical warfare. The 1944 RAF document "Plan for retaliatory gas attacks on Germany" recognised that the large scale use of chemical agents from the air was an untried weapon of war as far as the United Kingdom was concerned. Development of aerial chemical weapons and the production agents have been inhibited by the Treasury in the 1930s and its approval for retaliatory stocks was not given until February 1939. The RAF, which by 1936 had recognised that it was likely to be the principal user of the means of chemical warfare, had largely failed to prepare operational concepts. To a degree, it believed this was the result of the stronger War Office ie Army alignment with the British chemical warfare. The RAF had not had any great interest in chemical warfare planning. This dilemma continued to frustrate both planning and the production of agent for an untoward period, but by 1944 the RAF chemical agent and weapon stockpile was complete.

In the Army the stockpile was desperately small at the beginning of the war. There were 18,000 4.5 inch howitzer shell and 28,000 6 inch howitzer shell of the Great War type, both charged with mustard gas and some 500 tons of mustard gas and 5 tons of tear gas in the national stockpile. By the 19th April 1939 such munitions were with the British Expeditionary Force in

France; they were mostly brought back to the United Kingdom before the Dunkirk evacuation.

Gas munitions were developed for the Royal Navy during the Second World War but it seems that none were ever carried on ships; they remained in Royal Navy Armament Depots. The naval munitions were all shells from 4 inches to 8 inch calibre and charged with either phosgene, mustard gas or a tear gas. These were developed solely for the naval "support of landing operations for the purpose of harassing the enemy and forcing him to adopt anti-gas measures". The chemical warfare handbooks for the army of 1940 reflected the dated concepts and lack of chemical munitions for artillery; detailed instructions were provided on the deployment of the cylinder, now an essentially archaic chemical weapon. Fortunately, the defensive position was probably the best in any of the European forces. Provision of such equipment soon extended to the rapidly growing territorial Army, to militia training and, a little later, to the LDV (Local Defence Volunteers, later to become the Home Guard). Overseas garrisons were reasonably well equipped; and any deficits were soon made up. When Japan entered the war in 1941, the Imperial and Allied forces were faced with the prospect of using retaliation-in-kind and anti-gas defence on an almost world-wide basis. Japan was not a signatory to the 1925 Geneva Protocol and the Chinese had claimed that the Japanese Imperial Army had used chemical weapons against their forces on several occasions since 1937.

On 5 September 1939, two days after the outbreak of war, the Chemical Defence Research Department moved from Grosvenor Gardens in London to Porton, leaving a small rear party to maintain contact with the Ministry of Supply headquarters. By February 1940, because of difficulties in liaison with other departments the greater part of the London staff returned and were re-established in the Adelphi. Records and intelligence branches remained at Porton for some years; the latter returning to London in May 1943 and the former being absorbed by CDES.

Porton expanded considerably in the early months of the war, with an influx of scientists and technologists from the universities and industries. The mechanisms are now somewhat obscure but plans had been made by the Government for certain key scientists to join defence establishments on the outbreak of war. Other such moves were instigated by the senior academics and industrialists on the Chemical Defence Committee. Many distinguished scientists worked at the Establishment for periods during the war, including Professor G R Cameron the pathologist (later Sir Roy Cameron), Professor S Sugden, Professor H W (later Sir Harry) Melville, Dr

H M Carleton known to generations of histologists for his 1926 manual "Histological Technique", Sir Joseph Barcroft, C N Davies the doyen of aerosol research, Professor J H (later Sir John) Gaddum the pharmacologist and pioneer of probit analysis, and Sir Jocelyn Thorpe the eminent chemist. The actual number of CDES staff during the Second World War cannot be readily determined: it seems likely that total staff numbers were somewhere between 700–1000, including service men. Changes in organisation also occurred. During part of 1940-41 there was both a military Commandant and a civilian Chief Superintendent. In August 1941 the Commandant combined both roles. By 1942 the title "Commandant, Porton" had lapsed leaving the now military Chief Superintendent as effective head of the Station. This military post continued until 1948 when the title became a civilian appointment and eventually was re-designated Director in 1956.

Prototypes for the civilian respirator and the baby helmet; 1938.

On the declaration of war a London-based Territorial anti-aircraft gun battery was posted to Porton and manned several sites within the camp and on the range. In the event, Porton was never attacked. Many buildings were camouflage painted; the faintest residual pattern could in recent years still be seen on one or two buildings. Extra hutted living accommodation was built for the Officers Mess and for servicewomen. In fact, a rash of satellite huts appeared in all parts of the Station. Defensive pill-boxes were added to the corners of the "Closed Area": these have escaped listing in a 1985 definitive published account of pill-boxes "UK defences in 1940" by Henry Wills, a local author.

As the war in Europe developed the British Expeditionary Force in France fully expected to be confronted by German gas. In such a situation, as on the home front, many incidents were reported and investigated: Porton was the vital part of the evaluation process. False alarms continued to show the need for any use of gas by the enemy to be properly established and authenticated. Perhaps one of the most notable scares was the very widely accepted notion that in the autumn of 1940 the Germans were releasing some form of vesicant threads or cobwebs into the air over the United Kingdom. The Home Guard and ARP wardens seemed to have originated this concern. Studies at Porton soon confirmed the immediate scientific impression that these were not sinister secret weapons but a harmless natural phenomenon. One of the files of the period contains a copy of letter LXV from White's "Natural History of Selbourne" wherein the great naturalist describes similar unusual concentrations of airborne gossamer encountered on 21 September 1741; a poem entitled "Gossamer" written subsequently by some unknown member of the staff at

A small boy has been borrowed from somewhere to demonstrate the Second World War children's respirator.

GHQ Home Forces (then at Kneller Hall) in September 1940 contains the lines:

> "Security of home and health were shaking their pants
> Till Colville quoted a piece from White of Selbourne, Hants.
> They sent it out on all the wires "This matter's quite alright
> For any further references see letters, Gilbert White".

The arsine scare was somewhat less ludicrous and based on tenuous intelligence. Arsine or arseniuretted hydrogen (code-named Arthur) was a lethal, non-persistent agent with a systemic effect in destroying red blood cells. The Germans had always been keen on arsenical agents, the German respirator FE37 introduced before 1939 had been found to give high levels of protection against arsine and it was also learned that in the immediate pre-war period Germany had cornered all the available arsenic of the world metal market. The juxtaposition of these matters lead to the assessment that arsine might be used against the British Expeditionary Force. An auxiliary respirator canister (the Type EA) filled with specially treated absorbent granules was quickly provided for the GS respirator, being inserted in the middle of the corrugated rubber hose which connected the facepiece to the main canister. A special Detector Paper Type A was also developed; at Porton and rushed into service. Investigations after the war showed that fears had been unfounded. The high levels of arsine protection afforded by the German respirator were: fortuitous (being aimed at countering the threat of Russian hydrogen cyanide), and the arsenic stocks were for more general industrial use. That part of the stocks which was destined for chemical agent production was intended for the production of arsenol, which the Germans used as a diluent for mustard gas. The lessons from such events were well learnt and by 1942 when similar scares about German use of "Substance S" (HN2, one of the nitrogen mustard series) arose, the matter was better handled and the highlighting within the Army of any special threat was avoided. The "mirror-image" effect in the history of chemical warfare is well known and it is a salutary observation that the German perception of the sudden appearance of British detector paper for arsine, led them to assess that this gas must be a British agent of significance. This, in turn, led them to intensify their previously low level of interest in arsine.

Intelligence on the chemical warfare capabilities of the Axis powers was closely scrutinised at Porton and when the Chemical Defence Research Directorate headquarters returned to the Adelphi, its intelligence branch CDR5 remained at Porton until May 1943 under Major General Sir Henry Thuillier (Retd), who had been Director of Gas Services at GHQ in France and subsequently controller of the gas warfare branch of the Ministry of Munitions in the Great War. (Thuillier was the author of a 1939 book entitled "Gas in the next war" but which is curiously almost completely devoted to gas in the Great War). Unlike the situation in the United States America and Germany, there were very few openly available authoritative British texts on chemical warfare by former soldiers or officials, due to an attitude in the 1920s and 1930s that the public should not be disturbed by knowledge of the potential of gas in future wars. Open British publications, when they emerged at all, tended to appear in the medical literature.

All captured equipment was exploited in the laboratories and the fullest reports issued. The most commonly studied equipment's were Axis respirators; special interest lay in the performance of the charcoals and particulate filters in the canisters in the context of their vulnerability or indications of new Axis agents. Capture of chemical munitions was a rare event until the end stages of the war; all possessing nations took care to prevent such munitions falling into enemy hands. Some British chemical weapons, mostly Livens projectors, which had been taken to France by the No 1 Chemical Warfare Group of the British Expeditionary Force, were lost to the Germans at the time of the British evacuation. Further, certain British experimental devices and reports which had been given to the French, were discovered by the Germans when they over-ran the French chemical warfare laboratories at Le Bouchet.

What were the major concerns in the chemical field at Porton

A curious chemical weapon 1943; the frangible glass grenade: many ideas were evaluated and discarded during the Second World War.

A 1941 prototype for the "Installation Type A/LP" or Bulk Contamination Vehicle designed for the contamination of terrain with mustard gas. The white paper squares are being used in a trial with a coloured simulant to detect the extent to which the vehicle itself becomes contaminated.

during the war? Without doubt the greatest was to intensify the development of new chemical weapons and munitions; this had been started before the war in a desultory manner constrained by political uncertainties about retaliatory policy and compounded by lack of funds and resources. Hand-in-hand with this now accelerated development was the establishment of a section to plan and assess field testing and work with the operational requirements branches on battle-field tactics, munition expenditure and firing tables. Constraints on the scale of field trials at Porton were partly relieved by the collaborative efforts of Canada in setting up the Suffield Experimental Station in Alberta for conjoint use. Earlier Anglo-French plans to collaborate in trials at the French field trial facility in Algeria had foundered with the fall of France. The Suffield Experimental Station was established as a combined United Kingdom and Canadian chemical warfare experimental station in 1941. Originally ten scientists from Porton formed the core and were soon joined by Canadian staff. In June 1941 the Canadian Army became responsible for the site with Mr E Ll Davies of Porton as Chief Superintendent. Some 584 staff, mainly Canadian Servicemen, were at the Station at the end of the war. In 1946 British support ended and the Station was taken over by the Canadian Defence Research Board and became known as the Defence Research Establishment Suffield.

As the war progressed the number and range of chemical weapons and munitions which passed into service increased. By the end of the war in Europe the United Kingdom had appreciable stockpiles both at home and in theatres of war overseas. The United Kingdom's chemical agents, phosgene, mustard gas and a lachrymator (teargas): usually bromobenzyl cyanide generally termed BBC, were produced and weaponised in Agency Factories run by Imperial Chemical Industries for the Ministry of Supply, under conditions of secrecy and urgency. This association of industry and the Chemical Defence Research Department, notable through the station at Sutton Oak began, as far as the Second World War is concerned, in 1937. The main Agency Factory was at Randle in Cheshire; others were constructed at the Valley works at Rhydymwyn in North Wales and Springfields near Preston in Lancashire. Intermediates were produced at Rocksavage near Runcorn (which also produced phosgene), Wade near Northwich in Cheshire and Hillhouse near Fleetwood in Lancashire. Depots for bulk storage and ad hoc filling of RAF spray tanks were scattered throughout Britain: Army holdings of chemical munitions tended to be co-located with more conventional munitions. Between 1939 and 1945 3,394,093 Porton-designed 25-pdr base ejection shells charged with mustard gas were produced. In the same period impressive quantities of other calibre shells charged with one of the three standard United Kingdom agents were produced. For the RAF, bombs charged with mustard gas or phosgene and ranging from 30 lb. to 500 lb. were produced by the thousands. Nearly 60,000 spray tanks of various sizes were also produced. The total United Kingdom Second World War production of gas, both charged into munitions and weapons or held in bulk storage was 40,719 tons of mustard gas and 14,042 tons of phosgene and tear gases: the cost of such Production was £24M. Apart from these Army and RAF munitions and weapons, shells for naval guns, mostly of 4 inch and 4.7 inch calibres were designed and trialled. Stockpiles of such naval shells charged with phosgene were laid down in shore depots but none were carried on board HM ships. The only doctrine for naval use of gas shell was bombardment of land targets before or in support of landings. Whilst the naval stockpile was modest beside that of the Army and the RAF, a considerable development and trials programme at Porton was needed to fulfil Admiralty needs in an area where no real requirement had been stated until 1939.

Many experimental weapons and munitions were developed and trialled at Porton during the Second World War. Many were in response to Service requirements for chemical weapons specifically designed to attack armoured fighting vehicles, bunkers or pill-boxes. Others reflected efforts to increase the efficiency of aircraft delivery of mustard gas. Many such devices acquired local nick-names such as the "flying cow", "flying lavatory", "squirt" and "frankfurter". None passed into service because the requirement lapsed due to changing circumstances in specific theatres of war, or as the European and then Japanese war periods drew to an end, because of the diminishing likelihood for a need to retaliate in kind against the Axis.

The search for new agents was another major concern at Porton. Much was also done by extramural work at Universities, notably at Cambridge. When promising, new, highly toxic compounds were identified, several were taken to the stage of laboratory-scale production for field assessment but largely by the time important new classes of putative agents had been identified, the war had progressed to the stage where the lengthy process of development, trialling, developing production processes and scaling up to bulk production, was not considered worthwhile.

Smoke had been studied at Porton since the Great War, for screening, marking and signalling. The Second World War led to urgent operational requests for new smoke munitions and devices

A trial to evaluate the hazard from chemical shell in the 1950s. The shell will be fired from the inverted mortar seen suspended from the tower. Below is the target of white card surrounded by a grid of sampling devices and an arc of more sophisticated samplers.

Lord Louis Mountbatten watching a demonstration at Porton of smoke devices for possible use in the Dieppe raid. The date is not known but is probably the early summer of 1942. Air Commodore Combe, the Chief Superintendent skirts the unidentified senior officers behind Mountbatten. Lieutenant Colonel "Tony" Kent, then Military Experimental Officer, is largely hidden by the Grenadier Guards Officer in the foreground.

of all sorts, especially in coloured smoke for signalling and also the means to screen exceptionally large vital industrial targets at home. The needs of the Royal Navy for generating smoke at sea were long standing. For special operations such as the Dieppe raid, Porton smoke devices played a significant role, as they later did in the invasion of occupied France. The research on military smokes was relinquished by Porton in 1988-1989 and devolved to the then Royal Armament Research and Development Establishment near Sevenoaks, now DERA Fort Halstead. Over the last ten years, memories of research and development on military smokes have receded at Porton. The significance of smoke-creating munitions and other devices was once a major part of Porton life: a considerable number and diversity of smoke stores were developed and passed into Service between the Great War and the 1980s.

The possible retaliatory use of gas against the Japanese forces and the particular problems of defence against Japanese gas in tropical conditions was yet another problem of the period. The performance of impregnated clothing and anti-gas ointments under such conditions continued to be a weakness. Several agents, notably mustard gas, were more potent in tropical conditions. The development of an anti-gas ointment which would give skin protection against mustard gas for long periods in hot, sweaty conditions was eventually fulfilled by the development of Ointment Anti-gas No 6.

The impregnated clothing problem was more difficult. The

most-used British impregnite (2.4 dichlorphenyl benzoyl chloroimide) was named Anti-Verm (A subterfuge suggesting some anti-louse or insecticide property, employed for security reasons to avoid drawing foreign attention to the existence of British battledress impregnated with chemicals capable of neutralising mustard gas vapour). Inevitably, the Germans came to know of such matters when the British Expeditionary Force left France and British Anti-Verm socks were acquired. Impregnated clothing concepts had been a considerable preoccupation at Porton since 1935 and of interest from at least 1925. By 1938 co-operation with the dry-cleaning and textile trades had enabled a process which could be used for service battle dress in a standard dry cleaning plant. Impregnated battledress worn with a respirator was seen as the ideal alternative to encumbering troops with heavy impervious oil-skin clothing which could readily exact a physiological penalty under hot weather conditions or with arduous activity. Protection of the hands and feet was still needed, but this was not a major problem. Foot protection was initially by impregnated socks but later by the use of protective dubbin on boots. Serge battledress impregnated with Anti-Verm was stable in storage under temperate conditions. Under battle condition use, the protective properties remained for about three months. Laundering and dry-cleaning destroyed impregnite, so that a withdrawal and recycling process had to be instituted by the Royal Army Ordnance Corps, using special dry-cleaning firms. The scale of issue of impregnated battledress and, until 1940 socks, was impressive. All British and Commonwealth troops taking part in the invasion of occupied

Porton staff at the German chemical warfare station at Raubkammer bei Munster in 1945. Most, though temporarily uniformed, were civilians, who can be readily distinguished in this photograph by having no cap badges. The post-war exploitation of German chemical weapons at Raubkammer was particularly important. It was here that the British came across German 105 mm shells marked with three green rings, which on examination were found to contain remarkable potent and hitherto unknown organophosphorus nerve agent.

Europe were equipped with such clothing. Meanwhile, at Porton, thought was being given to the development of an impregnated "pantee" to protect the vulnerable groin area; the special problems of kilted troops were also studied.

The utility of Anti-Verm impregnated clothing in the tropics was one of the topics studies by a conjoint United Kingdom – United States – Australian team at the Australian chemical warfare laboratories and field stations at Prosperine and Innisfail in Queensland. It was found that under very hot and humid conditions the Anti-Verm was adsorbed through the skin to produce mildly toxic effects. This and the difficulties found in impregnating lighter cotton fabrics led eventually to the adoption of American impregnites and plant. When the war ended, impregnating companies were about to be raised in India, for which American plant was to be made available.

As the war proceeded, research on insecticides and repellents became important at Porton. The toxicology, physical properties and dissemination of DDT was given high priority from 1943. Impregnation of service shirts with DDT all but eradicated the perennial problem of lousiness in the field army: the first United Kingdom large-scale of production of DDT was at Sutton Oak. Medical aspects of war beyond those of chemical warfare were studied by Porton, including the effect of underwater explosions on immersed personnel, burn treatment, the hazards from explosive fumes in gun turrets, pill-boxes and tanks and from smokeless propellants.

With the advent of VE day, the trickle of senior staff returning to their pre-war posts began: the complement was cut by 10% and the Station programme revised. Inevitably, the future role of the Station began to be discussed, especially in the light of the fact that gas had not been used and the possibility that no nation had seen it as an essential part of military activity. Whilst discussions of such a sort continued in high places, they were disturbed by the British discovery in April 1945 in Germany of chemical shells bearing unknown markings. Examination of the agent charging revealed a highly toxic and (then) largely undetectable compound which could exert effects in a few minutes if inhaled or if the skin was contaminated. Further, exposure to non-lethal concentrations could produce severe and prolonged effects on vision. Subsequently this particular agent known to the Germans as GA, Tabun or Trilon 83 was found to be but one of a series of related compounds which the Germans had termed the G-agents and which eventually became more commonly known as the nerve agents. Concern about possible chemical warfare in Far East

Low-cost protection from aerial spray of mustard gas: a 1943 prototype, probably American.

Anti-gas protection of Service dogs was studied during the Second World War. A dog respirator completed the ensemble.

A 14 October 1943 Sunday afternoon demonstration of the decontamination and salvage of gas contaminated food at the Lido, Mansfield Road, Nottingham. Such conjoint Ministry of Food, Air Raid Precautions and Chemical Defence Experimental Station activity was frequent during the war years. Other venues included the Hurlingham Club, Bath cattle market, Watford football ground, the Stanley abattoir Liverpool and the NAAFI store at Amesbury.

theatres of war was relegated and almost the whole of Porton activity was now directed to investigation of the German chemical warfare capability, both by Porton and Allied scientists at the German chemical warfare facilities at Raubkammer and when samples were brought to Porton for detailed study. A vast programme of work on the nerve agents was mounted, both within Porton and extramurally with eminent contacts such as Professor Adrian (later Lord Adrian PRS) at the University of Cambridge.

During the few remaining months before V J day vigilance about a possible Japanese last-minute use of chemical warfare was maintained in the face of fastly-depleting staff, studies on the nerve-agents and the inevitable uncertainty about the future role of Porton. Gas had not been used; what then was its place in future wars? Had the nerve agents brought a new dimension to chemical warfare? What were the implications for any United Kingdom chemical warfare capability of the future? How were the new problems in defence, notably detection, prophylaxis and therapy to be solved? What was the impact of the nerve agent hazard on British military doctrine? Clearly, one of the major post-war tasks was to evaluate the German nerve agent munitions in the field.

The Second World War had seen great activity at Porton and by Porton or its London headquarters workers dispatched to India, Australia, Canada, South Africa and the United States. It is worthwhile recording the existence of the Chemical Defence Research Establishment in India (CDRE(I)), set up by Porton in 1929 at Rawalpindi and later at Wellesley Barracks at Cannanore from 1944–1947, with field trials areas at Porkal and Kumbala near Mangalore, and at Coimbatore and Trichinoploy. CDRE(I) pursued a programme, coordinated with that at Porton, on the problems of chemical warfare at chemical defence in hot and dry climates in the context of possible military action in India and the particular problems of the individual protection of often bearded and turbaned India troops. Much of the work in the CDRE(I) closing phases was on the use of DDT for control of insect vectors of infectious disease. CDRE(I) closed sometime before Indian independence in 1947. Porton activity in Australia was centered at Innisfail and the Australian Field Experimental Station at Prosperine.

These latter facilities were established by the Chemical Defence Board of Australia but the staff was augmented by both United Kingdom and United States staff, reflecting the joint United Kingdom and Australian responsibility akin to that which existed with Canada at Suffield. Essentially, this was an example of the Imperial and allied collaborative effort of the war years. The Chief Superintendent at Innisfail and then Prosperine was Lieutenant Colonel F S Gorril RAMC from Porton. About fifteen British officers and civilian scientists were stationed at Prosperine. In recent years claims that Australian Servicemen were used as human guinea pigs in trials with mustard gas have been sensationalised in both the United Kingdom and Australia by the media. A film "Keen as mustard" made by Briget Goodwin (later Brophy), based on archived film released in Australia did nothing to diminish concern. This was followed by her 1998 book "Keen as mustard: Britain's horrific chemical warfare experiments in Australia". In fact, the trials should be seen as essentially an Allied collaborative activity, albeit that the use of volunteer Australian Servicemen involved trials which would possibly not be seen as ethically or medically acceptable today. Notwithstanding, they provided definitive information on the enhanced hazard from mustard gas in jungle conditions.

Collaboration with South Africa was less expansive and centred around mustard gas production. Scientists from Sutton Oak were sent in small numbers to assist in the South African

The senior staff of the Biology Department at Porton in October 1943. Rear rank, from the left, Dr D Herbert, Dr G M Hills (in Home Guard uniform), Lieutenant J M Barnes RAMC, Lieutenant J M Ledingham RAMC, Dr D D Woods, Lieutenant (jg) USN MC, C Howe, Ensign H N Carlisle USN MC, and Lieutenant C E Venzke USA VC. Those seated, from the left, Dr G P Gladstone, Lieutenant W B Sarles USN MC, Dr D W W Henderson, Dr Paul Fildes, Dr J F S Stone, Lieutenant Colonel A Nimmo Smith and Lord Stamp.

mustard gas plants where the agent and chemical munitions were produced to United Kingdom specifications as part of the Commonwealth, Empire and Allied stockpile. The United Kingdom retaliatory capability had been developed after pre-war inertia and the means of defence improved. Undoubtedly these states of United Kingdom and Allied preparedness against possible Axis powers use of gas did much to influence the Axis decision not to use their considerable chemical warfare capability. Thus, the view emerged that the Allies in fact had won the gas war, without either side having recourse to this particular method of warfare.

Concepts of Biological Warfare put to the Test

The advent of the Second World War, intelligence; on more suspect activity in Germany, discussions with the Medical Research Council and communications with Sir Frederick Banting of Canada (one of the discoverers of insulin) caused the Committee of Imperial Defence to re-convene its original Sub-Committee on Biological Warfare. By February 1940, again under the Chairmanship of Lord Hankey, as Minister Without Portfolio in Chamberlain's War Cabinet, this became the War Cabinet Sub-Committee on Biological Warfare. The main need identified by the new Sub-Committee was for concepts to be devised and put to the test of experiment. In April 1940, the Sub-Committee was informed about exploratory work by France and in June Sir John

Ledingham reported on work on inhaled toxins by Dr D W W Henderson, a member of the staff of the Lister Institute. By September discussions between the Ministry of Supply and the Medical Research Council had resulted in arrangements for setting up at Porton a highly secret group to undertake a practical evaluation of biological warfare. This small group was to be co-located with CDES. It would rely on the many facilities and experience of the Station but would remain autonomous under its Director Dr Paul Fildes (later Sir Paul). Fildes reported initially to Lord Hankey as Minister without Portfolio and later to Mr Duff Cooper as Chancellor of the Duchy of Lancaster, though some token service involvement emerged later through the emphemisfically titled "Porton Experiments Committee" and the Chiefs of Staffs Sub-Committee on Biological Warfare. The Medical Research Council paid the salaries of the group and were reimbursed by the Ministry of Supply but otherwise played little real role in activities at Porton.

The group, which arrived at Porton in early October 1940, was called the Biology Department, Porton (BDP). The exact method whereby Fildes was selected is now obscure: it is certain that he had been consulted in earlier years. In 1959 he wrote that "I was invited by the MRC to undertake experiments on BW at Porton". His obituary almost gives the impression that he appeared before the earlier CID Sub-Committee and offered his services. Fildes was one of the foremost microbiologists of the era. He was 58 in 1940, a formidable, stern, dictatorial and highly respected senior medical man who had been a naval surgeon in the Great War and who since 1934 had directed the Medical Research Council Unit in Bacterial Chemistry at the Middlesex Hospitals' Bland Sutton Institute of Pathology. He was the third of the seven children of Sir Luke Fildes RA, a prominent Victorian artist who eventually became a fashionable and royal portrait painter. A life-long bachelor, he lived through most of his stay at Porton at the onetime Old George Hotel in Salisbury's High Street. Fildes and his group arrived at Porton surrounded by great secrecy, great import and the greatest priority, all of which tended to engender some local resentment. Fildes enjoyed brushes with authority and lost no time in publicising to Hankey any inadequacies encountered at Porton in his strenuous attempts to set up the group. Attempts by the Commandant and Chief Superintendent to integrate BDP more closely under CDES command and management failed. Bureaucracy was anathema to Fildes and he insisted that communication between himself and Hankey, and later Duff Cooper, was direct and exclusive. He also made it quite clear that decisions on the research programme were to be made by him and not by the Biological Warfare Sub-Committee. Again, in 1959 he wrote "The Chiefs of Staff did not direct the work. In fact, no one directed it except the scientists involved; the Chancellor of the Duchy of Lancaster was "responsible"". Fildes clearly demands more attention than he has hitherto attracted. Apart from several obituaries, an entry in the Dictionary of National Biography and uncollected memories in the minds of those who knew him, there is no major study of this intriguing man: this gap remains to be filled. His Royal Society obituary is probably the best and longest account of his life. It, like other sources, has led to the inference that his profoundly independent and iconoclastic views depended in no small way on his status as a "rich man". No-one can define "rich" of course, but birth in a large Kensington mansion, an education at a preparatory school, Winchester College, Trinity College Cambridge, the London Hospital Medical College in the last decade of the 19th century and the first of the 20th century, suggests at least a financially "comfortable" family background. However, recent information from Mr Paul Myers, his executor and husband of one of Fildes nieces, reveals that he had no capital until his father died in 1927, leaving him and his five brothers and sisters £10,000 each. Wealth came in later life, from the eventual sale of his interest in the British Journal of Experimental Pathology, which he had founded with three colleagues, the sale of his definitive collection of two-penny red postage stamps for £20,000 and a considerable interest in investments. For much of his early life, Fildes lived relatively frugally, off often derisory salaries. Fildes had always had wide interests. He had met Wilbur Wright through Alec Ogilvie, an undergraduate friend and an early aviator, often flying with Ogilvie in early aeroplanes. He had also assisted Ogilvie in his early work on experimental man-lifting kites in East Anglia. He was a talented furniture designer and cabinet maker, an expert in photography and in retirement a cataloguer of his father's drawings relating to his published book illustrations.

The modern use of monosodium glutamate as a flavour enhancer in the food industry is well known. When Fildes was at Porton during the Second World War, he noticed that when beef bouillon used in bacterial culture media became alkaline, it lost its flavour. He concluded that an amino-acid glutamic acid was responsible for the taste of beef. Unfortunately, he did nothing about this discovery beyond taking a bag of glutamic acid crystals to the Randolph Hotel at Oxford and telling them to put it in their soup. This suggestion was not well received. It was left to an American colleague to patent glutamates in the USA and make a fortune. Family genealogy was a great interest of Fildes in his retirement. He was particularly interested in the life of his great grandmother, Mary Fildes, who had been President of the Female Radical Reformers of Manchester.

Fildes was reputed to be a woman hater but, in fact he enjoyed their company and was particularly proud of his part in seconding the election of Marjory Stephenson, also a bacteriologist, to Fellowship of the Royal Society. In 2000 the new Medical Countermeasures building in the Sector was named the Fildes building in his memory. It is important to realise that BDP was, even with the exigencies of war which must have evoked many unconventional groups, a highly individualistic body. This charac-teristic continued well after the end of the Second World War and to a degree its successors, MRD and MRE, were always atypical Ministry Establishments.

Initially BDP consisted of less than a dozen medical men, scientists and technicians, most of whom had been enlisted by Fildes from his Medical Research Council unit or through personal contacts. Others including Dr D W W Henderson, soon to emerge as Fildes' deputy, came via CDES, at the instigation of Sir John Ledingham, from the Lister Institute. The staff eventually grew by the attachment of three or four scientists from CDES, the arrival of a few; RAMC officers and men, the local recruitment of junior staff and the eventual attachment of several American bacteriologists commissioned as US Army and Navy Officers. The total BDP staff probably never exceeded some 50 people of diverse origins and backgrounds, including a peer of the realm, a gamekeeper and, a member of the Forte hotel and catering family called-up into the Royal Army Medical Corps. The group was housed initially in a small complex designed as an animal house for the Physiology Section of CDES. Soon this was extended and linked to new hutted laboratories. The ground floor of the main BDP building then largely reverted to offices and workshops, leaving the upper floor as laboratories Above this a machine gun post for anti-aircraft defence was erected.

Fildes set out in his first report, before any experimental work had started, the ways in which he believed that micro-organisms might be used in war. Some such ways were identified as lesser possibilities for a variety of reasons. It was decided to concentrate on micro-organisms disseminated as an aerosol from bursting munitions or from sprays, and to examine the effects of inhalation of the aerosol the respiratory tract being eminently vulnerable to invading micro-organisms. Unlike the situation with chemical agents such as mustard gas, the undamaged skin was relatively proof against micro-organisms. Most chemical agents exerted their effects as gases, vapour or liquids. With biological agents, there were no gases or vapours; aerosol particles small enough to be carried through the air and thence deep into the lungs were produced from bursting munitions or from sprays. Firstly, methods had to be devised and evaluated in the laboratory and then in the field. Further, the infectious diseases that were of greatest significance had to be determined The design of bombs and sprays for dissemination leant heavily on CDES, which had nearly 25 years of experience in gas weapons. CDES also provided much expertise and facilities for field trials and in adapting laboratory production of microorganisms to semi-technical scales to provide enough suspension of bacteria for experimental bomb filing and trials.

By 1942 BDP had shown that several species of laboratory animal could be fatally infected by the inhalation of a defined quantity of spores of the bacterium Bacillus anthracis, the causative agent of anthrax. They had shown (using Bacillus subtilis, a harmless naturally occurring sporing bacterium isolated from hay on the Porton Range) that sufficient quantities of spores could be produced in the optimum range of aerosol particle size from bomblets and that a simulant agent cloud could regularly and reproducibly pass downwind from the bomblets at significant concentrations such that if the simulant were to be replaced by anthrax spores, then infection and death were sure to follow in animals and presumably in men exposed to the aerosol. Anthrax spores could not be safely released from bomblets or sprays on the Porton range but it was essential to show that munitions charged with anthrax spores would behave as expected and produce casualties under realistic conditions. Accordingly, the remote Gruinard Island (at the time known for security reasons as "X-Base") off the coast of Ross and Cromarty in Scotland was requisitioned as an isolated and safe site for trials and in 1942 and 1943 a team from BDP, assisted by CDES and Service staff conducted bomblet trials on the island. The story of these trials, kept secret for many years, has now become well known. The contamination of a small part of the island, the subsequent purchase of the island by Ministry of Defence until such time as the island was safe for man or beast and the eventual decontamination of the contaminated site using formaldehyde in sea water in the late 1980s after CDE had taken the initiative to solve the problem once and for all, led to the return of the island to civil use in 1990.

The Gruinard Island trials and a further single trial at a

Penclawdd beach on the Gower coast (which left no contamination because the site was subsequently washed by the tide) confirmed that sheep could be fatally infected under realistic conditions. It was deduced that deaths in personnel were certain to follow an exposure 200 yards downwind of the explosion of such a munition and that a serious risk extended for more than twice that distance. Further, on a weight-to-weight basis, the particular agent was 100-1000 times more potent than any then known chemical agent.

The United Kingdom made its data available to the US and Canada in pursuit of an Allied programme for a retaliatory biological capability in what was later to be called the "N bomb[6]" project based on 500 lb. cluster bombs containing just over 100 small 4 lb. bomblet sub-munitions of the type which had been trialled latterly on Gruinard Island Such clusters had been shown by the use of simulants in trials at Porton to produce an effective aerosol concentration of spores over nearly 100 acres from a small impact area. The United Kingdom had no large scale biological agent production plant, or indeed any sort of plant for pathogens, and no facilities for field trials with cluster bombs charged with the actual agent. Plans were made to produce anthrax spores in America and to trial charged cluster bombs in Canada. In the event, fulfilment of the Allied plans was halted by the end of the war, before the Vigo plant erected at Terre Haute, Indiana, by America, had produced any anthrax spores.

The immediate War Cabinet requirement for the United

---

[6] N was the BDP and later Allied code for anthrax.

The charging maching for depositing and sealing anthrax spores in cattle cake at Porton Down in 1942–1943. The open cakes pass from the right to the left side, receiving a charging of anthrax spores and then a seal of molten "bun" mix, before being oven dried.

Kingdom to have the means to retaliate-in-kind had however been fulfilled by 1943, by a weapon directed at livestock. BDP had determined that pending realisation of Allied plans for the anthrax cluster bomb, the only practical solution was a weapon requiring no special munitions or associated hardware, based on the charging of cattle-cake with anthrax spores and their subsequent delivery from the flare-chutes of bombers over the cattle grazing pastures of Germany. The cakes would be readily found and eaten by cattle; each contained a lethal ingestion dose of spores.

It was envisaged that retaliatory use of the stockpile of 5,000,000 cattle-cakes in "Operation Vegetarian" would strike a blow at Germany's already weak agricultural sector and, more importantly, underline the principle of retaliation-in-kind. The concept had been devised and trialled using mostly uncharged cattle-cake on the Porton Ranges and the numbers of cakes needed for aircraft flying at various heights and speeds to cover specific areas with the optimum concentration of cakes had been determined. The charged cakes were produced in a small building known colloquially, for reasons which are now obscure, as "Foyles factory" and built in 1941 for the ad hoc small scale production of various chemical and smoke munitions. Since the cattle-cake were also known as "buns" the building soon became the "Bun factory". The empty cakes were made by a well-known soap maker of Old Bond Street and supplied to Porton on a 250,000 a week basis: their manufacture from ground linseed meal being based on a modified soap tabletting process. Equally well known sweet makers and biscuit makers had been apparently unable to undertake the task. No great curiosity seems to have been evinced by the order for cattle-cake. Porton designed charging and sealing machines which could inoculate 12,800 cakes a day. The cakes were then dried and packed in boxes of 400. Production began 15 weeks before Christmas 1942 and the stockpile was completed by 22 April 1943. This capability, once the process was established was essentially run by one technician from BDP, 15 ladies from a Bristol soap factory who were employed at Porton during the war for ad hoc small production jobs, one laboratory assistant, two labourers and "one boy to assist". Apart from one or two boxes of cakes which were retained in the culture collection at MRD and MRE as memorabilia until 1972, the stockpile was destroyed very soon after the end of the Second World War. Whilst this particular weapon may not have been of outstanding military significance, it was as Fildes wrote in 1943 "developed as the quickest way in which we could make some retaliation at short notice". Its political significance is considerable: it is unlikely that any weapon of similar

Cattle-cake charged with anthrax spores.
The stockpile of five million cakes was stored in cardboard boxes, each holding four hundred cakes. The boxes were sealed with adhesive tape, with a metal ring to facilitate operational opening.

potential could be brought to operational availability with such simplicity, minimal resources and cost in its development and production.

BDP also did a little work for the wartime Special Operations Executive (SOE) on the feasibility of using substances which would ensure the lethality of non-lethal wounds from grenades and other devices. In this context, a trial was done in 1944 in a pill-box on the Porton Range where goats were exposed to a grenade containing metal fragments coated with botulinum toxin. The experiment demonstrated that lethality could indeed be assured from minor wounds. There is no evidence of earlier or later work on this topic but in 1982 Harris and Paxman in their book "A higher form of killing" asserted that the June 1942 assassination, by grenade attack, of Reinhardt Heydrich, the Nazi "Protector" of Bohemia and Moravia was successful only because the grenade or grenades used contained botulinum toxin and that they originated from Fildes at BDP. Whilst there are good reasons for the Czech assassins being supported by the SOE, Harris and Paxman provided no evidence and the connection between Fildes and the event is solely circumstantial and based on hearsay. The trial at Porton was two years after Heydrich's assassination. Further, German records provided no evidence that botulinum toxin was involved or indeed suspected. Thus, the matter of Fildes involvement, which appears to have been based on his reputed conversation with some unknown person at some undefined place and time, continues to be rediscovered at intervals from the 1982 book and re-promulgated. In reality, it remains one of the Porton legends and unless evidence appears, it is likely to remain so.

The apotheosis of research at BDP was to demonstrate the feasibility of biological warfare by all means short of actual use in war and to provide some way for the United Kingdom to retaliate-in-kind in the event of such use by the Axis powers. Besides these notable achievements BDP pioneered in several unique fields, notably the semi-technical scale of pathogen production, and in experimental airborne infection, thus providing some of the earliest United Kingdom effort in the then embryonic sciences of biotechnology and aerobiology. In the future, the successors to BDP were to become acknowledged leaders in such fields.

The Post-War Years

4

At the end of the Second World War the United Kingdom's capability for chemical warfare was considerable and manifest in an array of facilities. There were seven Ministry of Supply Agency Factories, conjointly designed by the Chemical Defence Research Establishment, Porton's sister Establishment, and Imperial Chemical Industries, for the production and weaponising of chemical warfare agents and for the production of agent precursors. These were at Randle, Rocksavage, Springfields, Hillhouse, Wade, Royd Mills and Rhydymwyn. The Chemical Defence Research Establishment, where process research for chemical warfare agent production was located, was at Sutton Oak, St Helens. Research development and field trials were centered on the Porton Down Chemical Defence Experimental Station. The London-based Controllerate of Chemical Defence Development managed all this activity and was inter-twined with chemical warfare and chemical defence staff in the three Services and the prestigious Chemical Board, soon to be re-established as the Chemical Defence Advisory Board under the Ministry of Supply's Scientific Advisory Council.

By 1945, the United Kingdom's capability had been based on three chemical warfare agents; mustard gas, phosgene and a tear gas, usually bromacetone phenone. The associated weapons and munitions included artillery shell and mortar rounds, aircraft bombs and aircraft spraying devices. The United Kingdom had produced during the war 40,719 tons of mustard gas and 14,042 tons of the other agents. Most had been charged into munitions and weapons eg 2,364,000 25lb base ejection shells and 711,640 aircraft bombs, all charged with mustard gas, had been produced by D-

A reunion of Second World War Portonians on 6 September 1946. Many senior figures are to be seen here, including the later Sir Owen Wansborough-Jones, A E Childs, Sir Charles Lovatt Evans, Sir Harold Hartley, Sir Fredrick Bain, Professor D D Woods, Professor J S Kennedy and Sir Paul Fildes.

Day. If chemical warfare had been used, the stockpile would have been replenished by the Agency Factories, whose total output was 900 tons of agent a month and the potential to produce 3,680 tons each month within six months' notice. Further, Commonwealth capabilities in Canada and South Africa, could have added a further 5,330 tons each month.

Notwithstanding this impressive capability, the immediately post-war situation was complex. The United Kingdom had become bound by its ratification of the 1925 Geneva Protocol to virtually a solely retaliatory policy. This considerably limiting factor had inhibited capability development in the 1930s and would do so again in the 1950s. Apart from the exigencies of war could the United Kingdom, justify maintenance of the capability in peacetime? Many factors affected the United Kingdom's view.

Chemical warfare had not been used in the Second World War. Was it clear why it had not been used? Was its utility waning? Was there a future for chemical warfare? Was chemical warfare now eclipsed by nuclear warfare?

The United Kingdom's experience of using chemical warfare and of being exposed to its use was now limited to the years of the Great War and was thus dated. The United Kingdom had no Chemical Corps and the Services had no traditional and assertively vocal focal point for this method of warfare. In fact, there was little enthusiasm in the Services: military life and doctrine would be simpler if chemical warfare did not exist.

On the other hand, the nerve agents developed and stockpiled by Germany during the Second World War provided great advantages to possessors and evoked seemingly intractable problems in defence. Further, the USSR was know to have rebuilt one of the German nerve agent plants in the USSR and undoubtedly possessed a nerve agent-based capability.

If the United Kingdom was to retain a capability it must be modernised to match the USSR threat: modernisation had to be based on nerve agents. There was thus a need for new process chemistry, a new pilot plant for nerve agents and the charging of munitions with a hitherto much more toxic agent. Doctrines of use would have to be planned. Ultimately a full-scale production and weaponising plant was needed. Further, the problems of defence against nerve agents were long-term and difficult.

The Nerve Agent Era and Abandonment of Offensive Capabilities by the United Kingdom

In the years immediately following the war there was little of the uncertainty about the future that had been evident at Porton after the Great War. Whilst chemical warfare had not been used in the Second World War and atomic weapons appeared to have eclipsed all else, the nerve agents were undoubtedly a major factor in ensuring that chemical warfare retained at least some part in United Kingdom military doctrine. It is perhaps difficult to appreciate the impact of these agents. Few earlier agents were quite so insidious. The well trained British serviceman was familiar with the characteristic smells of mustard, lewisite, chlorine, phosgene, BBC and KSK (ethyl iodoacetate): few of the older agents were odourless. A few whiffs of most of these at low concentration before the gas mask was donned would do little harm. However, with the highly potent, odourless, colourless nerve agents, able to exert rapid effects through skin, eyes and respiratory tract, no such latitude was possible. Demonstration of the actual effects of nerve agents on man and personal experience of the effectiveness of protective measures could not be built in to service training, as they were with the older agents. Unprotected men could not be put through gas chambers or allowed to see that if nerve agents were decontaminated swiftly from their skin no effects were exerted. Unlike

Surgeon Captain Archibald Fairley RN, Head of Physiology Section at the Chemical Defence Experimental Station during the Second World War and until 1951.

Old Porton from the air circa the early 1950s. The hutted part of the Microbiological Research Department is in the wood at the top of the picture. In the centre is the gas works where Mansfield oil gas was produced. A large number of huts remain from both wars and the new Engineering Section is seen in the upper right corner, near the Salisbury to London railway cutting.

most of the older agents, the margin between mild effects at low doses and death at higher doses was small: nerve agents could not be used in troop training. The problems of defence were now of a new sort. Equally, development of a United Kingdom chemical warfare capability based on nerve agents brought other problems in future production by industry, weaponising, trialling and stockpiling. Military usage and the role of nerve agents in differing types of warfare had to be considered in detail.

At Porton, the Station now had a civilian Chief Superintendent, Mr A E Childs. (A civilian Chief Superintendent post was created in 1941 to parallel the Military Commandant. When the title of Commandant was dropped in 1942, the Chief Superintendent post became military). In February 1948, the directorship of Porton was vested for the first time in a civilian Chief Superintendent, a title which continued until 1956, when it was changed to Director. Childs, a physical chemist, had been at Porton since the early 1920s becoming successively Head of Chemistry Section in 1938, Deputy Superintendent of Experiments in 1940 and Superintendent for Research and Development from 1941–1942. In 1949 he returned to London as Director of the headquarters Directorate where he had spent much of the war as Principal Technical Advisor to the Director. He continued to serve on several official advisory bodies during the 1950s.

In 1948 there was the expected post-war departure of personnel from war work to the universities and Industry. Staff numbers contracted from the over a 1000 complement of the war to about 800 in 1953. Superimposed on staff problems were the massive lack of modern facilities and the effects of the ravages of war-time shortages and lack of repairs and upkeep. However, in the subsequent era of post-war austerity and continued shortages, followed by defence cut after defence cut, the wonder is that the Establishment survived at all.

Despite the desperate preoccupation with the nerve agents, diverse new roles were being adopted and lodger units became a feature of life at Porton. Towards the end of the Second World War in 1944, responsibility for military use of DDT fell to the Chemical Defence Directorate and Porton; control of the malarial mosquito in the Far East and elsewhere had become a major problem for British and Imperial troops. Porton established an entomology section under Dr (later Professor) J S Kennedy FRS where work on locusts, mosquitoes, flies, bed bugs, lice and all insects of military importance could be done. Full-scale field trials involving DDT spraying from aircraft over mosquito-ridden areas could not be undertaken by the Ministry of Production. Because of the expertise and facilities at Porton and the analogies between pesticide dissemination and chemical warfare Porton was eminently suited for such a role. This work was subsequently co-ordinated by the Colonial Insecticides Committee under Professor Sir Ian Heilbron. The Colonial Office Anti-Locust Research Centre, South African departments, the International Red Locust Control Service and Porton subsequently mounted trials in Tanganyika in which eight Anson aircraft sprayed the Porton formulation of the pesticide DNOC, with highly successful results. In 1948 the Colonial Office stationed its own research unit at Porton with the tide Colonial Office Pesticide Research Unit. CDES still maintained its own small entomology section for a few years but the Colonial Office unit was maintained at Porton with many changes of title; the last being as an Overseas Development Natural Resources Institutes unit which left CDE's Closed Area for its new home at Chatham in April 1990. The impact of Porton's role in pesticide research and development is still an under-recognised historical topic.

In 1947 the Medical Research Council set up its new Toxicology Unit within the main Physiology Section at CDES under Dr J M Barnes, who had served as an RAMC officer in BDP during the Second World War and who, until his untimely death, was widely regarded as an outstanding toxicologist. The unit pioneered research in the toxicology of organophosphorus pesticides, beryllium, plasticisers and other agricultural and industrial hazards but in 1950 moved to Carshalton and thence in recent years to Leicester, where it still continues. The Medical Research Council (known as the Medical Research Committee until 1920) had been involved with chemical warfare matters since the Great War and through its own Chemical Warfare Medical Committee had published at least eighteen major reports and an "Atlas of Gas Poisoning". The Medical Research Committee was represented on the original Chemical Warfare Committee by notable men of medicine and science such as Sir Henry Dale and J B S Haldane. It continued to be peripherally involved with matters of chemical defence (and later biological defence) until some time in the 1950s. Occasionally it instigated unusual ad hoc activity at Porton. In 1945 the Medical Research Council had been asked by the War Office to investigate the possible hazard to personnel from operating Radar. It was subsequently agreed that this would be done under the aegis of the Medical Research Council at Porton, with Professor J S Young of Aberdeen University Pathology Department and Professor G R Cameron of University College Hospital, London providing the histological expertise. The work was classified Secret and given the deliberately obscure title of the "High Frequency Dehydration Project". Accordingly rats were exposed in different ways to the emanations from Radar equipment parked outside the Physiology Section and run by a unit of the Royal Electrical and Mechanical Engineers. The final report on the study was presented to the Council in 1947 and demonstrated the unlikelihood of Radar operators being affected in any way by radiation. The tradition of both ad hoc studies in fields remote from chemical defence and of lodger units continued. In 2000 within the Sector these include Hunting Engineering Ltd, the National Institute for Biological Standardisation and Control, the Science Park and CAMR's Fermentation Plant.

The advent of the nerve agents had indirectly emphasised the inadequacies of Porton's ageing facilities and the inappropriateness of the layout of much of the camp. Porton had grown higgledy-piggledy without much consideration of safety, logic or aesthetics. The traditional Porton small, scattered, individual buildings increased fuel and maintenance costs and encouraged the isolation of small autonomous groups. In 1947 Edgar Bateman who had been at Porton since 1922, was Head of the Technical Chemistry Section during the Second World War and then after a period in London returned as Superintendent of the Field Services Division and later became Deputy Chief Superintendent, prepared a plan for the "modernisation of toxicological warfare" embracing both chemical and biological fields. What has since become known as the Bateman Plan was intended to rebuild the facilities at Porton and Sutton Oak over a number of years on a compact and orderly basis and to enable the range at Porton to be used more effectively for trials with highly toxic material. Housing and similar facilities were also included. The plan was approved but inevitably defence economies caused the postponement and then the indefinite shelving of the plan. Bateman was killed in one of the Comet air crashes in 1953, aged 52. The only parts which were implemented were modern engineering workshops, the siting of what was later to become the MRE on land adjacent to CDEE and the provision of Ministry of Supply housing estates in Salisbury. Aesthetics have played little part in the evolution of Porton, where economy and functionalism in architecture have predominated but in recent times many eyesores have been removed or tidied up. The programmes of tree and shrub planting which were started by the long defunct Ministry of Works, the Defence Land Agent and the Property Services Agency, the Defence Estates organisation and the site ground maintenance contractors in recent times, have enhanced the surroundings considerably. The woods which stretch from the Idmiston Arch entrance to the old Mess and the avenues planted in the 1930s which line the principal roads within the older areas of the Establishment are now mature. Those avenues which were planted in the early 1950s to line the new road running from the then CDEE past the new MRD building have also now achieved a considerable effect.

A major but little known task was imposed on Porton in 1945. This was the writing of a series of reports on chemical warfare and chemical defence as a part of the Ministry of Supply Permanent Records of Research and Development during the Second World War. Some 86 monographs on chemical warfare topics were called for but many were never written or remain as drafts. At least 23 of those that were published are available in the Public Record Office. Surprisingly they are rarely referenced by authors.

As after the Great War, in the years after the Second World War, where the exigencies of the nerve agent programme permitted, the Establishment turned to remedy deficiencies in basic research, especially the theoretical and experimental investigation of the diffusion of particulates over long distances, the physics of aerosolisation of liquids and powders, absorbents, filter theory and a detailed study of the biochemistry of the nervous system.

As research on the nerve agents progressed, the Services and the Home Office, equipped with Porton's assessment of offensive potential and the hazard arising from use against British troops and the civil population, could now issue their formal requests for the types of nerve agent-based munitions and for the new protective measures they required. On the offensive side, GB, known to the Germans as Sarin, emerged as the particular nerve agent on which UK chemical weapons were to be based. A series of bombs for RAF use was required. The Army requirement centred around a 25 lb. shell and a munition for the 4.2 inch mortar. Later in the 1950s when the V-series of nerve agents was discovered, there was Service interest in air and army weapon systems for the dissemination of the even more toxic VX, a low volatility, thick, oily liquid with remarkable percutaneous toxicity, considerable penetrative powers and the ability to persist on contaminated terrain or equipment for days or weeks. In the event, development work at Porton and at Nancekuke for the future United Kingdom chemical warfare capability in the decade after VJ day led to nothing because of the 1956 decision to abandon chemical weapons. Nevertheless, and most importantly, this post-Second World War excursion into the realms of offensive thinking and preparations, gave us an excellent understanding of how other nations could use similar chemical weapons against the United Kingdom and its forces.

On the defensive side, service requirements were stated for a real-time detector for nerve agent in the field, shipboard detectors for RN vessels, prophylaxis and therapy for nerve agent poisoning, a new Service respirator, collective protection for specific facilities, ships and vehicles, the means of monitoring decontamination and the residual contamination of terrain and equipment. The procurement cycle for some such items was relatively quick. For others the process was one of continuous improvement through several Marks reflecting advances in science and technology. In the 1950s–1960s the Establishment possessed a large self-contained engineering department heavily committed to development work and with highly specialised areas for rubber and polymer technology, textiles, and the design of plant and weapons. At one time, twelve engineers, fifteen drawing office staff and eighty mechanics staffed this important and then large part of the Establishment.

In 1949 Childs was succeeded as Chief Superintendent by a biologist, Dr H M Barrett, the Head of the Canadian Experimental Station at Suffield This two year posting was in the nature of an exchange; Dr E A Perren of CDES being appointed to take Barrett's place at Suffield. It was largely at Barrett's instigation that twin 22 feet diameter test spheres were built at Porton, to provide containment in which to study agent aerosols produced by bursting munitions. These have recently been demolished.

By late 1951 Barrett had been succeeded as Chief Superintendent by Mr S A Mumford, who had joined the Station in 1923 and became successively Head of Chemistry Section and Superintendent of the Research Division. Mumford had been engaged in his early years on the chemistry and physical chemistry of mustard gas. With the advent of the Second World War he became the leading authority on practical problems of detection, protection and decontamination and made notable contributions to anti-gas matters in the ARP Department. He was also largely responsible for the development of effective means of using the insecticide DDT in South-East Asia Command in the latter stages of the Second World War.

When Mumford retired in 1955 he was succeeded by Dr Perren, the post of Chief Superintendent being replaced by that of Director in 1956. Perren, who continued as Director until retirement in 1961, was essentially a research chemist of high calibre, who had come to Porton in 1922, became Head of Technical Chemistry Department in 1941, Superintendent of Development Division in 1947 and was the Head of Chemistry Section and Superintendent of the Research Division until 1955. When Perren retired as Director in 1961, he returned to the laboratory and spent several years studying a range of highly toxic chemical compounds. Perren is also remembered for his extensive activities in the post-war intelligence exploitation of the German chemical warfare capability.

Most areas of the Sector have seen major changes since the end of the Second World War. Fundamental studies on aerosols which became the major role of the old Physics Section and later the Physics Division, have waxed and waned: there is now no such Division though "aerosol" was retained for some years in the title of the onetime Detection and Aerosol Division. Smoke studies, once another major facet of life have disappeared. The supply of experimental animals, which during the war had been the responsibility of the Royal Army Veterinary Corps, was from 1949 catered for by the Animal Farm, which for some years from 1954 became known as Allington Farm, Porton and for rather more years was an autonomous Establishment with its own Superintendent and an intensive agricultural role in cereals, sheep and beef cattle. This later reverted to its parent Establishment. Its progress resembles that of the former outpost at Nancekuke in Cornwall which was once an autonomous Ministry of Supply facility as the Chemical Defence Establishment, Nancekuke, from 1953–1961, when it became part of CDEE, Porton and eventually closed in 1979.

The Chemical Defence Establishment, Nancekuke 1951–1980

The facility at Nancekuke near Redruth in Cornwall, opened in 1951 as a replacement for the Chemical Defence Research Establishment at Sutton Oak, St Helens in Lancashire. The latter was no longer considered suitable. Between the wars CDRE was a sister establishment of what is now the CBD Sector at Porton Down, being the focus of research and development for process production at laboratory, semi-technical or pilot-plant scales, an essential preliminary before any large scale chemical warfare agent production could be started. During the Second World War, such large-scale production was at the Agency Factories set up and managed by Imperial Chemical Industries for the Ministry of Supply, The discovery of the highly toxic nerve agents meant that the pilot-plant production of such agents could not be studied at CDRE because of its situation within a built-up area, with houses within 250 metres of the facility. Accidental release of nerve agents from the facility would have exposed nearby residences to extreme

The nerve agent pilot plant at Nancekuke's "North Site" in the mid-1970s. The plant was decontaminated and partially dismantled in 1956. It was completely destroyed in 1977–1979. The building to the right of the stack was the stabilisation plant. It also contained a shell-charging unit which was never used except with a simulant.

hazards. Accordingly, from 1947 a new site was sought in a more isolated area of the United Kingdom. By 1947 the former RAF Portreath airfield at Nancekuke was taken over from the Air Ministry in July 1949 and the partly demolished and decontaminated CDRE at St Helens was handed over to the Ministry of Supply Lands Department for sale in 1954. The site was eventually completely demolished and now forms part of a civil light industry site. From 1956, the role of Nancekuke became essentially defensive. Research centered around the assessment of how chemical warfare agents might be produced by future belligerents, studies on the intrinsic chemistry of diverse agents, the preparation of special chemical compounds, detector papers, powders and paints, the production of therapeutic and prophylactic drugs, development of charcoal cloth and anti–riot control agents and the destruction of batches of old chemical warfare agents. A reduction in staff numbers ensued. In 1959, on the dissolution of the Ministry of Supply, CDE Nancekuke came, like CDEE, under the aegis of the War Office. In April 1962 it ceased to exist as an autonomous establishment and became a part of CDEE becoming, firstly its Process Research Division and then in 1975 its Process Chemistry Division. As part of the Defence cuts announced in the 1976 Defence White Paper, it was decided to transfer part of its programme to the then CDE, together with some staff, and to close the facility. Between 1976 and 1980, an extensive closure plan was implemented involving the decontamination and demolition of buildings, the disposal of dismantled equipment, the safety clearance of remaining facilities and the redundancy or transfer of staff. The facility closed on 30 September 1979 with the emergence of a second RAF Portreath. The site is still an RAF Station.

Porton has never been immutable or rigidly fixed: it has always sought to move with the times. In fact, it appears to be in a constant flux, punctuated by brief periods of stability of role, complement, and aim. Inevitably, most flux has been occasioned by external political factors though there is a small tradition of internal reorganisation throughout Porton's life, which on closer inspection seems generally to have served no real purpose. The incorporate of CBDE into DERA stimulated the greatest organisational change for decades.

To provide a succinct history of even the first 20 post-war years is difficult. Firstly, there is too much to summarise effectively. Secondly, there are a few topics which for reasons of national security, cannot be fully reported. Thirdly, there are many recent aspects which cannot yet be seen in their proper perspective. The first 20 years or so of the post-war period at Porton can be characterised by the change to civilian directorship, by the pre-occupation with the nerve agents and on a national and policy basis by the abandonment of both the offensive research programmes and the production plants and weapons to retaliate-in-kind in the face of chemical attack in any future wars.

The Rise and Fall of Biological Warfare and Defence

In the aftermath of the war, as with CDES, there was a rapid exodus from BDP. Fildes, now knighted for his wartime services, and most of the senior staff returned to their institutes or university laboratories. D W W Henderson, who had been Fildes' right hand man remained. Ostensibly he was still a member of staff of the Lister Institute but with Fildes' backing he remained at Porton. In January 1946 with Henderson as Chief Superintendent, BDP became MRD, still co-located within CDES, still a well defined autonomous unit but continuing to rely on CDES for many services and collaborating with CDES on many aspects of research and development.

David Henderson

Like Sir Paul Fildes, D W W Henderson (1903-1968) was a powerful and memorable figure, who was involved with micro-biology at Porton Down from the summer of 1940 until 1968, some four years after his formal retirements as Director of MRE. His personal research output in terms of written work, from 1929 to 1967, was not large, amounting to some 28 papers. However, his influence on world-wide contemporary microbiology from about 1946 was immense, through his influence as Chief Superintendent of MRD and later Director of MRE. After graduation at the West of Scotland Agricultural College in 1926, he went to the University of Durham, then to the Lister Institute of Preventative Medicine in 1931, both at Chelsea and Elstree. He gained his PhD in 1934 and a DSc a year or so later. By 1940 he was working part of the time at the Chemical Defence Experimental Station at Porton but soon transferred to Fildes Biology Department, Porton, where he rapidly became Fildes deputy, initiating laboratory work on aerosol infection with anthrax and major collaborative effort with the US Chemical Corps Biological Laboratories at Camp Detrick for which he was awarded the US Medal of Freedom, Bronze Palm. In 1946 he became Chief Superintendent of the MRD and by 1956 Director of MRE. In 1951 MRD moved into its new laboratory building which was undoubtedly the foremost of its kind in the world. Thereafter, Henderson was able to stimulate and encourage his staff to vast levels of performance and to extend the scope of MRE far beyond BW defence. In 1955 he described the research activities at MRD in a lecture to the Royal Society. In 1959 he was elected to the Fellowship of the Royal Society. After his 1964 retirement as Director he continued to work at the bench at MRE until 1967, when illness made this impossible. In 1953, soon after the death of his first wife, he married Emilie Helen Kelly, an American bacteriologist who had been his assistant at Camp Detrick during visits in the Second World War. They moved from the old Camp Commandant's house at Porton to a 15th century cottage, "Swaynes Living" on the banks of the Avon at Great Durnford, where Henderson created an immaculate garden. Henderson was one of Porton's most forceful and dynamic senior scientists who evoked great devotion from his staff. He was undoubtedly patriarchal. Although often overbearing, he was protective of his staff and created an environment where each could give of their best. Henderson's posthumous portrait in oils, by Kohler, taken from the photograph in one of his obituaries, hangs in the ante-chamber of the lecture theatre at CAMR along with photographs of the successive Directors and Chief Executives of MRE and CAMR. In 2000 the Sector named its new micro-biological containment building after Henderson and in his memory. CAMR perpetuates his memory by the Henderson Memorial Lectures, started in 1975 and continued near-yearly.

The success of the trials on Gruinard Island and research in subsequent years by the United Kingdom, the United States and Canada, had convinced the Chiefs of Staff and the Government that further study of biological warfare was essential. Though the development of a United Kingdom nuclear weapon capability had a profound effect on military doctrine, biological warfare was still, for a few years, perceived to be of great significance and the need for the United Kingdom to possess a retaliatory capability had not diminished. Ultimately, this need started to diminish from 1951. In the period of post-war austerity, what great value was attainable by diverting money from nuclear weapons, where there were no controls on first use, to chemical and biological weapons, where the United Kingdom had adopted reservations in its ratification of the 1925 Geneva Protocol which meant that such weapons could be used solely in retaliation-in-kind? The retaliation-in-kind concept became an unacceptable basis for major weapon systems, however efficient. This change of policy took a few years to evolve but eventually it became clear that the United Kingdom could not afford the luxury of pursuing both offensive chemical and biological weapons and nuclear weapons. By 1956–1957, all research at Porton Down was based on the United Kingdom's solely defensive policy, decided at the Cabinet Defence Committee meeting on 10 July 1956 under the chairmanship of Sir Antony Eden. Curiously, the record of this meeting refers solely to chemical weapons. Some have surmised that biological weapons were subsumed under chemical weapons in this instance but it is quite clear that the offensive biological warfare programme was being run down before the 1956 meeting and the programme rapidly became essentially defensive. The contemporary importance of biological warfare was reflected in the construction of a vast new £2.25 million building for MRD adjacent to the senior Establishment. Building began in 1948 and MRD moved to its new location in the summer of 1951. The construction of this new Establishment in a period of extreme austerity and pre-occupation with nuclear weapons emphasises the perceptions of the military utility of biological warfare which existed in earlier years. Early United Kingdom post-war policy, albeit slipping away, was still orientated around the eventual production of 1000 lb. cluster bombs charged with anthrax for RAF use. No immediate Army or Navy requirement was apparent, though the distant prospect of rocket-type missiles with cluster warheads was noted. Several other agents had shown promise. The fundamental requirement was identified as detailed and long range study of the processes underlying biological warfare and defence: the ad hoc weapon studies necessary in the war had no place in the United Kingdom programme of fundamental research on the growth of bacteria, the behaviour and detection of bacterial aerosols, pathogenesis, microbial genetics and immunology. Experimental biological weapon design devolved to CDES, which by 1948 had become CDEE.

Staff recruitment for MRD was initially slow; microbiology was something of a new discipline and well qualified workers were scarce. Henderson's reaction was to recruit the most able scientists he could find, irrespective of their degree subjects and send them to his former colleagues and friends at the Post Graduate Medical School or the Lister Institute in London for appropriate training. Such unorthodoxies required support in high places since they involved much disruption of normal civil service practices. Henderson disliked bureaucrats and looked for high level support of a more independent nature. In 1946 he wrote to Fildes telling of the intent that a high level advisory body be created and stating that he had "complete assurance that there will be no stooge in the Ministry who will control or direct the work of my Department". In 1946 the Ministry of Supply Advisory Council on Scientific Research and Technical Development (later the Ministry of Defence, Defence Scientific Advisory Council) set up a new constituent body, the Biological Research Advisory Board (always described colloquially as "BRAB") under the chairmanship of Lord Hankey and with distinguished members such as Professor E C Dodds (the distinguished biochemist and physician, later Sir Charles Dodds), Sir Paul Fildes (now returned to the Medical Research Council), Sir Howard Florey (of penicillin fame, and later Lord Florey), Lord Stamp (one of the original BDP staff who had

The newly-opened Microbiological Research Department at Porton in 1951.

The library at the newly opened Microbiological Research Department (later the Establishment and since 1979, the Centre for Applied Microbiology and Research). The seated figure is Corrine Denham, who joined in 1948. This quality of library accommodation was unheard of in Ministry laboratories.

spent most of the war years on liaison duties in the US and Canada; by now Professor of Bacteriology at the Post Graduate Medical School) and O H Wansbrough-Jones (later Sir Owen) representing the senior and sister Chemical Defence Advisory Board. Departmental representatives included the Principal Director of Scientific Research (Defence) and Henderson. In time the BRAB grew bigger under the successive chairmanship of Lord Hankey and Sir Charles Dodds, only to wane because of policy change under the chairmanship of Sir David Evans, and eventually disappeared before the closure of MRE in 1979.

The move to the new building took place in the summer of 1951. Advance parties had gone ahead to set up MRD's miniscule administrative offices. The laboratories moved in phases, over a period of about a month, using now rarely seen RAF "Queen Mary" long-load vehicles. The vacated buildings reverted to CDEE use, though after some years the hutted laboratories were demolished. "Foyles factory", which had become the BDP and then MRD animal house, was eventually converted into laboratories.

One of the earliest MRD activities was to commission plans by CDRE at Sutton Oak and CDEE engineers on the design of a pilot-plant for studies on the means whereby bacteria might be produced on a large scale. This was eventually built in and around the hangar of a onetime Tank Armaments Research (a lodger unit) outpost on "Gas Compound Road" leading to the long gone remains of "Gas Wood". None of the CDRE or CDEE engineers were familiar with microbiology but they were knowledgeable on contained plant. Equally, none of the MRD staff involved initially knew much about microbiology. Most were industrial chemists, who were soon dispatched by Henderson for training elsewhere. Eventually the MRE pilot plant and its staff were recognised as world leaders, especially in the safety containment of microbial plant and in continuous culture. The plant was taken over by CAMR, with the main MRE building in April 1979.

Despite the emphasis on broad-based and fundamental studies at MRD and MRE, there was considerable pressure from the Chiefs of Staff, through the Inter Services Sub-Committee on Biological Warfare to evaluate the behaviour of agents and munitions in the most realistic way through trials in the field, as had been done on Gruinard Island. Largely, MRD took the view that it was necessary to know the mechanisms underlying phenomena, rather than merely know of their existence; a necessity usually fulfilled by painstaking laboratory work, rather than against the traditional background of meteorological uncertainties and vast resources and personnel removed from the laboratory to distant trials locations for months on end. However in 1948 MRD with the support of the Chiefs of Staff, BRAB, CDEE and the Services, began Operation HARNESS, the first of five major trials which were carried out at sea. Gruinard Island was now seen as unsuitable on several counts, notably safety limitations caused by wind direction and the proximity of the mainland. Some search was made for an alternative island site in United Kingdom waters but in the end it was decided to explore the use of the sea as a range. Trials at sea would not be restricted for safety reasons by latitude and wind direction and there would be no contamination of terrain, pathogenic micro-organisms would be diluted to extinction by the sea and the air, and also sunlight would be a factor in destroying infectivity. The essentials of such trials were the dissemination of agent aerosols from a bursting munition or spraying device carried on a float, situated up-wind of an array of air sampling devices and animals in an arc of rubber dinghies. The factors affecting particle fallout, virulence and viability could be evaluated and compared with results obtained under laboratory conditions. In later trials the techniques became modified and a section of a "Mulberry harbour" was used as a pontoon instead of the array of dinghies.

Operation HARNESS (1948–1949) took place in waters off the Leeward Islands "to determine the practicability of conducting BW trials at sea"; using greater distances than on Gruinard's land with three bacterial agents ie Bacillus anthracis, Brucella suis and Francisella tularense. It confirmed the practicability of sea trials and the utility of certain bacteria other than anthrax as agents.

Operation CAULDRON (1952) was held in May–September off Stornaway in the Isles of Lewis with the aim of consolidating data on Brucella suis gained in Operation HARNESS and to assess the utility of a further bacterium, Yersinia pestis.

Operation HESPERUS (1953) was also done in Scottish waters to consolidate data on Francisella tularense and Brucella suis and to compare the efficiency of several munitions and sprays.

Operation OZONE (1954) saw a return to the West Indies, at Green Cay to acquire more data on spraying bacterial agents and for the first time, on a virus, Venezuelan equine encephalomyelitis.

Operation NEGATION (1954–1955), also at Green Cay, compared the loss of viability in two aerosolised bacterial agents, and Venezuelan equine encephalomyelitis A second virus, Vaccinia virus, as a simulant for smallpox was also used.

The magnitude of these trials over nearly a decade, like the scale of the MRD building, serves to remind us of the status and priority once accorded to biological warfare and biological defence research. The 4,000 ton tank landing ships HMS BEN LOMOND and HMS NARVIK, which had been re-fitted as floating laboratories for these trials, were eventually laid up and later broken up. Sea trials with pathogens on the same scale eventually became an impossibility, due both to diminishing resources and the lack of impetus due to gradual abandonment of United Kingdom aims to develop a retaliatory capability.

After the removal from CDEE to the new MRD building, the inauguration of an influential BRAB, the success of the early sea trials and staff increases, MRD increased its international status, not only in the biological warfare community but as a centre of excellence in several areas of microbiology and allied disciplines. Its success was undoubtedly due to Henderson's driving force and his long held view that the two major pitfalls to be avoided were developing a rigid organisation and attacking a too wide range of problems. Whilst MRD work initially still had a very high priority, reflecting the Chiefs of Staff intent that biological warfare research should equate to that on atomic energy, Henderson still had to fight to obtain the resources that he deemed essential. Sir Owen Wansborough Jones (a former Chief Scientist of the Ministry of Supply) described Henderson as having "an innate distrust and general contempt for authority and the establishment, which he did nothing to conceal . . . but who always recognised his duty nationally and so long as he could continue exploring fundamentals, never overlooked his special and peculiar responsibility". Lesser luminaries and MRD staff had great regard for this patriarchal figure, often tinged with some apprehension about his ready shows of displeasure.

By 1957 the infectious levels for at least 15 species of microorganisms had been determined and a great understanding of the factors affecting airborne travel of aerosol particles and of the mechanisms of inhalation infection had been achieved. Significant progress had been made on the chemical nature of virulence, continuous culture, aerobiology, immunochemistry and bacterial genetics and a start had been made on the newer discipline of virology. The indication from earlier sea trials that the strategic potentials of biological warfare were considerable and hitherto unappreciated, was of great significance. Subsequent trials by CDEE and MRE, using inert particles of zinc cadmium sulphide or harmless micro-organisms as simulants, showed that the strategic deployment of biological warfare against the United Kingdom or United Kingdom forces posed an immense hazard and that a prime need existed for an early warning device for biological agents in the atmosphere. Other research showed the considerable potential for clandestine, unattributable sabotage and small scale attack by biological agents in a wide variety of situations.

In 1957 MRD became MRE and the title of Chief Superintendent was changed to Director, thus according the same status to both major Porton Establishments. 1957 saw other changes at Porton, notably the departure of the Royal Artillery battery and the take-over of the barracks by the local offices of the Ministry of Public Buildings and Works. The period also brought a gradual abandonment of aims to develop an offensive capability in biological warfare (and to destroy all existing chemical agent stocks and abandon the programme to produced a nerve agent based chemical warfare capability). Nancekuke began the run-down immediately but at MRE, where the accent had always been on research, rather than development, no specifically offensive research was underway. Very few MRE staff had been involved with offensive matters since the Second World War, and as far as MRE research was concerned, the policy change had no immediate effect. Nevertheless, it was to be of profound importance in the future.

The Last Four Decades 1960–2000

5

Whilst this period is characterised by the solely defensive role adopted by the United Kingdom, it is paradoxically a period of mounting concern about the chemical and biological threat, about actual use of chemical warfare in several nations, about almost explosive proliferation of chemical and biological warfare capabilities in many areas of the world, and the increasing offensive potentials arising from developments in science and technology. These concerns were concurrent with increased momentum for the Chemical Weapons Convention, with the Biological Weapons Convention of 1972 linked (again paradoxically) with a subsequent increased perception of biological threats, an enhancement of the biological hazard (through recombinant-DNA technology and biotechnology) and with the United Kingdom focus for biological defence at Porton devolving from MRE to CDE. The complexities of describing the last four decades are considerable. The Kent history finished in the late 1950s and there is no single source of summarised later activity at Porton that can be used.

Into the Ministry of Defence 1960–1970

In 1959 the Ministry of Supply was disbanded and CDEE, together with MRE, Allington Farm and Nancekuke passed to the War Department. By 1961 the Establishment at Nancekuke had become the Process Research Division of CDEE. Parts of the peripheral east and south-east areas of the range were let, for the first time, to local farmers. Building continued and by 1965 the Establishment possessed new chemistry and physics buildings. In 1964 CDEE and MRE passed into the newly constituted Ministry of Defence. The 1960s were marked also by high level studies on chemical and biological defence needs under the Chairmanship of Sir Alexander Todd (later Lord Todd), by the American military use of the riot-control agent CS in Vietnam, the reputed use of chemical warfare by Egypt against Royalist factions In the Yemen and by the use of CS in Northern Ireland by the police and the army. On the arms control front and in the political arenas of several nations, matters connected with chemical and biological warfare were attracting increasing attention and continued to do so from the 1960s. Arms control alms, high level consideration of chemical and biological defence policy, the use of CS for internal

Part of the Chemical Defence Experimental Establishment in the 1960s: much of the detritus as of the war years has gone and the growth of trees has done much to enhance the appearance.

security and allegations of chemical warfare in various parts of the world were all eventually in various ways, to exert effects on activities and events at Porton.

Despite the abandonment of aims for an offensive capability and the exclusive commitment to defensive research at Porton, suspicion and opprobrium continued in Parliamentary and public circles. This was however of little concern to most at Porton. The tradition of heaping abuse on Porton and Portonians was after all well established; the press was an ever-ready means. Magazines such as the now defunct "John Bull" and "Titbits" seemed to have been particularly fascinated by Porton in the 1920s and 1930s e.g. "Our Poison Gas Men: the Truth" in "John Bull" of 7 October 1933. Recruitment was undoubtedly affected by opprobrium and Ministers were rather more sensitive than Portonians. To some extent successive post-war Governments had contributed to unease and suspicions. Secrecy had always attended decisions on matters of chemical and biological defence and the decision unilaterally to abandon retaliatory chemical warfare programmes was made in secret and unrevealed until the 1980s. The "protective measures only" policy was not made evident for some years and even then was not clearly stated Probably the first definitive Ministerial statements were made in 1968 and 1969 when open weeks were held at MRE and then CDEE (and at Nancekuke in 1970) to clarify roles and to demonstrate that the United Kingdom policy in was solely one of defence, and that no secret facility for production of chemical or biological weapons existed or was envisaged. Thereafter the level of abuse diminished, demonstrations at the

Porton establishments fell off considerably as the Committee of 100 and other factions lessened their interest in Porton.

Accidents and fatalities had always exacerbated public unease and Ministerial anxieties. The death of an RAF volunteer, Leading Aircraftsman Ronald Maddison, during nerve agent experiments at CDEE in 1953 and the 1962 death of an MRE scientist, G A Bacon, from an accidental plague infection had considerable repercussions at both Establishments in terms of improved and tightened, ethical, medical and safety requirements. Local authorities were often prompted by individuals or factions to undue concern about the possible effects on adjacent villages of release of chemicals or micro–organisms if there was to be an air crash on the Porton campus. Anti–vivisectionists were another faction who had targeted Porton since at least the early 1920s. All these manifestations of unease about Porton combined almost insidiously to evoke changes over the years.

The value of "gas" for riot control or police work had been apparent in America and several continental nations for nearly half a century. In the United Kingdom, there was little interest, although in the colonial police services of the Empire military tear gases had been available and occasionally used, for many years. No such use occurred in the United Kingdom until that of CS in August 1969. This resulted in concerns which led eventually to the Himsworth enquiry on the medical and toxicological aspects of CS.

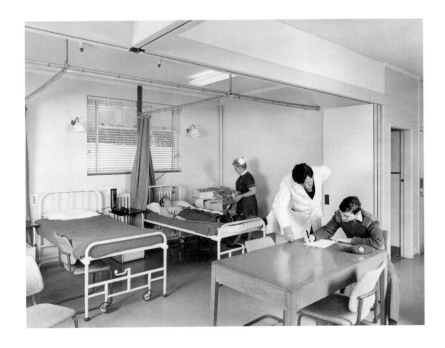

Porton Down volunteers in the 1970s in the Establishment's hospital. The white–coated figure is Group Captain R J Moylan-Jones RAF.

Sir Harold Himsworth initiated years of studies at Porton, leading to many official reports and several dozen open publications in the scientific literature by Porton staff. The Himsworth reports of 1969 and 1971 in effect vindicated MOD's earlier selection of CS as a more effective and safer replacement for the old tear gases such as choracetophenone (CAP or CN). CS was first synthesised in America in 1928 but it was not investigated at Porton until 1934 when it was screened as one of many possible military lachrymators or tear gases. CAP had also been used for years in many nations in military training, as a useful simulant for unpleasant or lethal war gases e.g. in respirator testing. However, it was not ideal for riot control and in the mid 1950s a search for something better began. Attention at Porton turned to some of the tear gases screened in the 1930s and CS was, after several years, accepted as a military replacement for CAP in 1958 and production studies begun at Nancekuke. The production of CS as both a military training aid and riot control agent for police use was transferred to civil industry in the late 1980s. In recent years the adoption by many British police forces of CS for police protection has caused a resurgence of interest, particularly the hazard posed by a new solvent adopted by the current civil industry, methyl isobutyl ketone. Again, the Sector has been involved in toxicological appraisals.

The Establishment also became increasingly involved in trauma studies. It had engaged sporadically in such work since at least 1937 and later continually in the context of the fulfilment of internationally agreed obligations to limit the injury potential of small arms bullets. The Colt Armalite rifle had been used against British forces in Malaysia, producing wounds worse than formerly encountered: the Establishment subsequently studied its effects. Later still, the Establishment was tasked to the need to establish and limit the injury potential of a range of weapons and devices, notable the baton round systems. All these activities involved close contact with other Establishments and the Services Medical Departments. Body armour, biochemical aspects of trauma and surgical problems were also studied at Porton and continued on matters arising from the Falkland's campaign and more recently from the Gulf hostilities, where the prospect of chemical agent-contaminated or infected wounds posed not only an increased hazard to the victim but a risk to medical and surgical teams.

In the mid-1960s, there were reports that Egyptian forces had used chemical weapons against royalist factions in Northern Yemen. Assessment of information on lethal and other effects and analysis of reputed residual chemical agent at Porton proved (like the United Nations investigations) somewhat inconclusive; those few samples reaching the United Kingdom showed only residues of tear gas. Nevertheless, it was clear that some more potent lethal agent must have been used and that establishing the validity of reputed chemical warfare in far-off places, let alone identifying the agent involved, was no simple process. In 1965, United States forces in Vietnam started to use the harassing sternutator DM and the tear gases CN and CS against Viet Cong troops (The United States declared that their use was not contrary to the 1925 Geneva Protocol. Further, the United States had not then ratified the Protocol and was not bound by it). This use, and the use of defoliants in Vietnam, contributed to the increasing world wide concern about chemical and biological warfare.

Mr E E Haddon became Director of CDEE in 1961. He had been at the Chemical Defence Research Department HQ in London since 1929 and by 1943 headed its CDR branch which dealt with the development of antigas equipment. Later he became Personal Assistant to the Controller of Chemical Defence Development (Mr J Davidson Pratt). By 1952 Haddon was Assistant Director of Chemical Defensive Research and Development and by 1957, when Childs retired, he had become Director of the London HQ. Much of the post-war re-equipment of the Services for chemical defence arose from Haddon's efforts, both in London and later at Porton.

On 27 May 1966 CDEE's 50th Anniversary was marked by a visit from the Duke of Edinburgh. This was the first visit of a member of the Royal family since that of King George V in 1918. Unlike the first visit, there are still documentary and film records of

The Microbiological Research Establishment's pilot-plant and the Chemical Defence Establishment's Motor Transport Section sometime after 1960. The trees on the right were the residue of "Gas Wood" of the Great War. The dark brick building was the site of Experimental Plant No 2, designed for pathogens but never used as such.

the 1966 royal progress at CDEE and MRE. With the Chief Scientist Ministry of Defence (Army Department), the Deputy-Master General of the Ordnance, the Director of Biological and Chemical Defence, the Director of CDEE and the Director of MRE, the Duke met senior members of the scientific staff and the senior Service liaison officers, listened to presentations on research projects and saw the equipment under development for the Services. Much the same programme was repeated at MRE; some interesting detail has survived. At MRE the Duke of Edinburgh's car door was opened by Mr J L Smith, the Head Messenger and former NCO of the Royal Artillery, wearing Ministry messengers uniform, peaked cap, white gloves and medals. Some informative facts on the protocol for use of Royal Standards and the Union Jack in the context of flag poles fixed to buildings and free-standing flag poles have also been preserved. The 60th Anniversary of CDE in 1976 seems to have attracted little attention, possibly because defence economies had called into question the very future of both the Establishments at Porton. However, Defence Public Relations staff produced a brief historical account of CDE in the form of a Diamond Jubilee folder which was used to jacket the Establishment brochure or any other printed ephemera of the period.

1966 also saw the "Mercury" computer installed and the old gas retort house converted into a laboratory. (The Establishment had for long had its own gas works, producing the distinctively smelling Mansfield gas from oil. Somewhen in the early 1960s, "town gas" reached Porton). 1968 brought an exacerbation of the international unease, when an aircraft spray trial at Dugway Proving Ground in the United States went awry and the nerve agent was disseminated off-target, resulting in the death of many hundreds of grazing sheep and the eventual need to destroy the whole flock of 6,000. An accident with VX also occurred at an American base in Okinawa, resulting in the hospitalisation of 23 US troops. Such incidents together with the American use of chemical agents in Vietnam increased the domestic and international opposition to United States chemical and biological warfare research and weapons programmes. Much of this opprobrium rubbed off onto the United Kingdom because of research collaboration with the US.

On the retirement of Haddon as Director in 1968, Mr G N Gadsby was appointed to the CDEE Directorship. A onetime chemist, he was commissioned into the Royal Warwickshire Regiment and later posted to the Royal Military College of Science at Shrivenham, where he continued to lecture as a civil servant. After posts at the then Army Operational Research Establishment, he became its Director. Later, he was appointed to be Director of Biological and Chemical Defence (by then the much diminished London headquarters for the Porton Establishments and Nancekuke). At the time of his appointment to Porton, he was Deputy Chief Scientist (Army) in the Ministry of Defence. Gadsby's Directorship was marked by much international concern about chemical and biological warfare, national concern about the riot control agent CS and notably, in 1969, a week of open days at CDEE. The Porton profile was substantially raised during this period Mr Gadsby's directorship was notable for the enhancement of assessment and operational analysis work, which took place at his instigation. Mr Gadsby was appointed to a senior post in the British Defence Staff in Washington in 1972.

By 1969 President Nixon had been moved to abandon the United States biological weapons capability, review policies on the chemical weapons capability and announce his intention to sign the coming Biological Weapons Convention and to submit the 1925 Geneva Protocol to the Senate for ratification: the United States eventually ratified the Protocol in 1975. The Nixon renunciation announcement on 25 November gave the reasons for the decision to abandon the United States capability as the "massive, unpredictable and potentially uncontrollable consequences" associated with biological warfare. However, this abbreviated rationale was not reflecting a view previously extant in the United States throughout the quarter of a century of offensively related policies and research. In recent years, after a decent interval, scholars are beginning to say that the decision was essentially political, to draw attention away from the longer established and proven chemical capability recently used in Vietnam, to placate congressional, national and international concern, and to enable the United States to make progress in arms control. Domestic political considerations were the main motivation and British proposals to separate chemical from biological warfare in arms control efforts provided an opportunity for discarding unilaterally a whole method of warfare with maximum publicity and minimal penalties. Regrettably, the Nixon rationale has been reiterated over the years since 1969, as if the United States had suddenly become aware of some hitherto unperceived feature of biological warfare of sufficient magnitude to render it militarily useless. This false rationale bedevilled biological defence efforts for decades. The conjoint effect of the 1969 Nixon renunciation and the advent of the 1972 Convention was synergistic. As biological warfare became unmentionable, it tended as a threat to become invisible. This dangerous lack of perception was almost fatal for biological defence research progress in several nations.

In its last two decades the MRE had two well defined roles: to assess the hazard of biological warfare and to devise the means of protection of the Armed Forces. This was, for many of the staff, a matter of fundamental research, where the link between topic and the role of the Establishment was tenuous. For others, it was more obvious and direct. MRE attracted many leading scientists whose interest in defence matters was limited: they were drawn to MRE by its reputation and its superb facilities. The accolade of acceptability had been given by much open publication of MRE work and by the presence of eminent figures on BRAB. Gradually, the majority of MRE scientists became engaged on work which was not in reality directly aimed at biological defence. As the inevitable and regular defence economies impinged, the integrity of multi-disciplinary teams at MRE could only be maintained by undertaking work beyond the defence role. Budget cuts could be off-set by money from the civil sector. When Henderson retired in 1964, the situation appeared erroneously to be stabilising. It was accepted that the interests of the Establishment should widen. The facilities and expertise were without parallel and the similarity of many problems, whether they arose from some future use of biological warfare or whether from naturally occurring disease, led to work on behalf of the Ministry of Health, the Medical Research Council, the Public Health Laboratory Service and industry. The new Director Dr C E Gordon Smith brought further esteem to the Establishment by establishing it as a centre for arbovirus research and the investigation of urgent international public health problems such as the pathogenesis, identification and therapy of dangerous new infections such as Vervet Monkey Disease, Ebola Fever and Lassa Fever, and in the production of a wide variety of microbial products. Such work also gave MRE the opportunity to enhance its world leading status in microbial safety practices.

In 1968 a series of open days at MRE served largely to dispel some of the lingering suspicions that the United Kingdom policy was not confined to solely defensive work. Openness had always been a feature of the Establishment. In contrast to the necessary constraints placed upon CDE, most MRE work was unclassified and results were published openly in the scientific journals. Certain results of the wartime work by BDP had been published openly just after the war. By the mid-1970s 90% of the work was being published and by that time over 2500 scientific papers or lectures had been written or delivered by MRE staff.

More Economies and Uncertainties' and the Demise of the Microbiological Research Establishment: 1970–1979

In 1970 the word "Experimental" was dropped from the Establishment tide, which was then to remain as CDE for the next 21 years and thus constitute something of a record, given the avidity with which titles had changed over the decades. The reason for the 1970 decision is now quite obscure. In the same year the Technical Information and Records Section was re-housed in a onetime laboratory and workshop block and a well-equipped lecture theatre arose within the shell of its earlier building. A large and modern animal house for the Medical and Biology Divisions was also erected on the site of the now demolished hutted laboratories which had been used for biological warfare research by BDP during the Second World War and later, until 1951, by its post-war successor the MRD. By 1971 changes were afoot in Whitehall: CDE now became an Establishment within the Procurement Executive of the Ministry of Defence. CDE's depleted headquarters, now in the Adelphi and the successor to the 1951 Chemical Defence Research Department, which latterly had been the Directorate of Biological and Chemical Defence (DBCD), became the Directorate of Research, Chemical and Biological (DRCB). It was under this title that it continued until its demise in the 1979, when the tradition of a London headquarters which had been extant since the Great War, came to an end.

In 1972 Mr Gadsby was succeeded as Director by Mr T F Watkins, who had joined the then CDES in 1936. In 1939 he was seconded to the Chemical Defence Research Establishment in India and later headed the Research Divisions at Sutton Oak and Nancekuke. From 1956 he had been Head of Chemistry Section at the Establishment and later Deputy Director of CDEE. In 1973 Allington Farm became a CDE Division; in later years the farming and laboratory animal breeding sides were separated into smaller units. A year later the Establishment's new ballistics facility for trauma studies was commissioned and on 1 July 1975, Lord Zuckerman, a former Chief Scientific Adviser to the Ministry of Defence, who was one of the pioneers in this field, notably on blast injury, made a formal visit to hear presentations and inspect the equipment in the facility. The Establishment's standing in this particular field of military medicine was now considerable and valuable contributions were (and still are) made to the surgical treatment of British casualties in Northern Ireland, the Falklands war, Kuwait and elsewhere. By 1976 a review of the future of chemical and biological defence at the two Porton Establishments was again under way; economies were once again being sought and uncertainty prevailed. The United States ratification of the 1925 Geneva Protocol, the abandonment of the United States biological warfare capability, the coming into force of the 1972 Biological Weapons Convention, the threat from the Warsaw Pact and above all the need to slim programmes, reduce resources and save money, were all, often conflicting factors which affected the review. One consequence of the need for reduction in the defence budget was the seeking by CDE, and more so by MRE, of income from civil work: at one time the income at MRE from such work defrayed over 25% of the annual cost of the Establishment. The future of MRE had been a particular problem since the dissolution of the Ministry of Supply in 1957. The transfer to the War Department had been opposed by both the Director of MRE and the Biological Research Advisory Board of the Defence Scientific Advisory Council on the basis that the future welfare of the Establishment and its contribution to both biological defence and general microbiology could only be secured under civil control as a major national scientific asset; with the assurance of stable, long term control unaffected by the fluctuations of defence policy and spending and without the "Service" label which was identified as deterring recruitment of the best staff. This view, presented to the War Department in 1960 did not prevail but was considered by the Todd Panel in its major review and later by an interdepartmental working party and at the highest levels in other departments. By 1970 the Ministry of Defence had agreed to continue biological defence research at MRE at the same level for at least a period of five years, before re-appraising the situation in the light of events.

However, by the mid-1970s, most grave considerations on the very future existence of MRE were afoot. Dr Gordon Smith had been succeeded in 1971 by Dr R J C Harris, who was unwittingly to preside over the slow demise of the Establishment. The factors contributing to the decision to reduce the level of effort on biological defence and to close MRE are numerous, complex and interactive: they have been touched on earlier in this publication. In some ways MRE had subscribed to its own closure as a Ministry of Defence establishment by venturing into non-defence research. It had been encouraged to do so by BRAB, the venture had massive public relations bonuses and it had achieved the stated aim of retaining unique multi-disciplinary teams within the Establishment. At the same time, this had evoked a fall-away of awareness on matters of biological warfare in other areas, an official realisation that a large Ministry of Defence Establishment was less than fully

John D Morton OBE, the mastermind behind the biological trials conducted at sea from 1948–1955. He later became an American citizen.

committed to Service requirements and even much official debate of the need for any United Kingdom effort on biological defence. All these factors interacted synergistically.

The 1970s were consequently a period of increasing unease at MRE. By the mid-1970s it had been decided that a reduced programme of biological defence research was acceptable and that this would be done by the transfer of a small team from MRE to CDE. The Central Policy Review Staff were invited to conduct a study on the possible future civil use of the staff and facilities of MRE, to ensure the perpetuation of a national centre of excellence in microbiology. The Medical Research Council was then asked to lead in a detailed review of the capability of MRE for civil research. Ultimately, the announcement was made that on 1 April 1979 the staff and facilities of MRE would be transferred to the Public Health Laboratory Service and become the Centre for Applied Microbiology and Research. The transfer of a small focus of expertise to continue biological defence studies would be enabled by the concurrent creation of a Defence Microbiology Division (DMD) within CDE.

For CDE, the possibility of being extinguished was more remote. Although chemical agents had played no part in a European war since 1918 and had not been used in the Second World War, they were perceived to pose not only a hazard but a specific threat to NATO. To continue chemical defence at some level was desirable, despite the need for concentrating resources in

Histological work in the Experimental Pathology Section of the Microbiological Research Establishment in the 1960s or 1970s.

support of the "teeth" of the forces. This wisdom was later endorsed, as further aspects of not only the chemical threat from the Warsaw Pact emerged but of chemical capabilities in several potentially hostile and other nations. Notwithstanding, by 1974 a defence review of exceptional ferocity was in hand and by 1976, the decision had been taken to cut the budget for the Porton establishments, to close the CDE Process Research Division at Nancekuke and ultimately to close MRE and transfer responsibility for a much diminished biological defence role to CDE.

In May 1974 Mr Watkins retired as Director of CDE and was succeeded by Dr R G H Watson who had earlier been Director of Naval Research and Development Administration and from 1969 Director of the Admiralty Materials Laboratory at Holton Heath. On 30 September 1979 Nancekuke closed. The Officers' Mess, which had existed at several sites at Porton since 1916 closed at the same time as MRE. In 1979, a large new extension of the CDE chemistry facilities was started.

Biological Defence 1979-to the Present

The role of the onetime Defence Microbiology Division (DMD) was initially to maintain a focus of knowledge, advice and expertise relevant to biological defence within the Ministry of Defence and to act as a watchtower for significant developments in microbiology and other relevant sciences which might lead to a change in the threat CDE had no special facilities for microbiological work, especially that involving the use of pathogens. Inevitably, for the new DMD, housed in part of a building designed for physics research, the setting-in process was slow and frustrating. The DMD role was almost immediately expanded to include CDE's newly acquired responsibility for Gruinard Island. The problem of Gruinard Island had remained unsolved for decades. Bad images of several sorts had sprung from it. The owner had sought the return of the island in 1945 but the Ministry of Supply refused de-requisition on the grounds that the island was still contaminated as a result of wartime experiments and could not be returned until it was deemed safe. At that time due to great sensitivities about such matters the nature of the continuing contamination was never officially stated: when it inevitably became known, the opprobrium increased considerably. To allay the owners continuing concern the Crown had agreed in 1946 to purchase the island: when the contamination no longer existed the owner or her heirs would be able to re-purchase the island for the sale price of £500. Accordingly, the island was inspected yearly from 1947 to 1968 by a party from MRE and samples of terrain collected for the assay of the anthrax spores. No progressive diminution of the spores was found. Ways of removing or sterilising the islands top-soil had been studied in the 1970s but these were immensely costly or environmentally unacceptable. In 1978, in anticipation of CDE taking over responsibility a small joint CDE and MRE team made a survey. This was followed by a series of detailed visits and studies from 1979 to 1985 which re-addressed the question of the extent of the contamination and how decontamination of the terrain could be achieved. The contamination was found not to be widespread as had previously been assumed, but virtually limited to the immediate area of the wartime munition deployment. The prospects for decontamination were now much more encouraging. Improved techniques for the quantitative determination of anthrax spores were developed. Experiments were done to find the most practicable and efficient sporicidal chemical. A solution of formaldehyde in sea water eventually emerged as the disinfectant of choice. The Institute of Terrestial Ecology advised on ecological acceptability.

The importance of the matter and the years of public debate and unease suggested that an independent body should maintain an overview of CDE's studies and plans. Accordingly the Independent Advisory Group on Gruinard Island was set up with the involvement of the President of the Royal Society under the Chairmanship of Professor W D P Stewart FRS (now Sir William Stewart), then Boyd Baxter Professor of Biology at the University of Dundee, subsequently Secretary of the Agriculture and Food Research Council and from 1990–1995 the Chief Scientific Adviser at the Cabinet Office. CDE's conclusions on the efficacy of disinfection through irrigation of the contaminated area with a solution of formaldehyde in sea water and the identification of an appropriate contractor were endorsed. In June to August 1986, the decontamination was carried out. Tests to determine the efficacy of the decontamination were made in October 1986; these showed a few isolated residues of anthrax spores and re-treatment was done in July 1987. Further tests in October 1987 showed that all onetime positive sites were now yielding negative results. The indigenous rabbit population was examined for antibodies to anthrax; none were found. To demonstrate confidence in the decontamination procedure a flock of sheep was grazed on the island from May to October 1987, visited daily by a shepherd and his dog, and monthly by the District Veterinary Officer. There were no ill effects. Reseeding of the treated areas resulted in a luxurious growth of grass. Taking all the facts into consideration the independent advisors concluded that "the chances of persons or animals contracting anthrax on Gruinard Island are so remote that the island can be returned to civil use". At a ceremony on the island on 24 April 1990 the Under Secretary of State for Defence announced that as the island was now "fit for habitation by man and beast", the Ministry of Defence would return the island to the heirs of the previous owner on 1 May 1990. Nearly 50 years after the island was used to meet the desperate exigencies of war and 11 years after the custody of the island passed to CDE, the island was back in civil ownership.

DMD continued meanwhile to formulate a biological defence research programme. Research had begun on rapid detection and identification methods for agents, on the anthrax bacillus, microbial toxins and on selected arboviruses. Work with certain pathogenic micro-organisms initially involved the use of CAMR facilities, pending the adaptation or construction of new laboratories at suitable safety containment levels.

In the mid-1980s two matters combined to cause a further reappraisal of the level of biological defence effort. There were increased manifestations of the threat and the proliferation of biological warfare interest and activities in several nations was particularly alarming. The opportunities now provided by the development of recombinant-DNA technology (one of the aspects of the popular term "genetic engineering") and massive developments in industrial microbiology for large scale production of micro-organisms and microbial products were assessed as enabling a massive advance in biological warfare. Further, a detailed look at the threat showed that these opportunities were now being explored elsewhere in the world. Subsequently, with the support of an independent advisory group (which though not directly subordinate to the Defence Scientific Advisory Council, as BRAB had been, was of similar status) the Ministry of Defence embarked on an enhancement of the biological defence programme at CDE, by building up a team of scientists within DMD to establish recombinant-DNA technology, identify priorities for its application in biological defence and assess how nations with a biological warfare capability might misuse the technology in improving their offensive programmes. The enhancement of DMD occurred during the 1980s and resulted in an increase in scientific staff. By 1987 14% of the Establishment's staff were employed on the biological defence programme; by 1988-1989 this had risen to 17% and subsequent to the Gulf conflict was estimated to be about 30%. Developments in molecular biology and "genetic engineering" are now being applied to assessments of biological hazards, rapid identification of agents and new vaccines. Biological defence is pursued energetically not only in the present microbiology area but in Departments concerned with detection of aerosols, with assessment and with field trials. As recorded elsewhere in this booklet, biological defence advice and equipment were prominent in the Establishment's support for Operation GRANBY in the Gulf War and those senior people of BDP once concerned with the first experimental study of the realities of this means of warfare at Porton during the Second World War would have been impressed with the speed and quality of the ad hoc support and advice provided from Porton.

The Establishment had provided support to the Foreign and Commonwealth Office for the successive Review Conferences of the 1972 Biological Weapons Convention since 1979. Original staff of DMD who came from MRE, latter day DMD staff and former MRE staff now in other areas of the Sector have played, and continue to play a prominent part in detailed studies on developments in science which might affect the scope or the effectiveness of the Biological Weapons Convention and in analysis of States' Parties involvement in several Confidence-Building Measures, providing data on national activity and facilities of relevance.

Despite great vicissitudes over the years, support for arms control measures and research leading to the provision of effective protective equipment, drills and advice for the Services continues the tradition established in biological defence research over half a century ago, albeit that the option of retaliation-in-kind no longer forms part of the UK policy or programme. In 1991 plans were made for a new building within CBDE to house the major part of DMD's pathogen-handling laboratories and containment suites and so release the earlier adapted and ad hoc structures acquired in the early years of DMD for more suitable purposes. In 1999 this building, named in 2000 the Henderson Building, was completed. It is a little paradoxical that biological defence at Porton should have returned in 1979 to the "Closed Area" of CBDE, where biological warfare research began nearly 40 years earlier and that MRE, once dedicated to such research, should have been absorbed by the Public Health Laboratory Service, a body originally founded for biological defence before the Second World War. MRE and its precursors had, from 1940–1979 only four civilian Directors. Most defence establishments changed Directors frequently: during the same period CDES and CDEE had been headed by 13 soldiers or civilians. Fildes died in 1971, Henderson in 1968, Harris in 1980 and Gordon Smith in 1991.

There is some evidence that some desultory bacteriology was done at Porton in the Great War for checking the safety of the camps water supply. This apart, microbiology at Porton is only 60 years old. Nevertheless, and whatever Porton Establishment has been or is involved, Porton continues to be internationally acknowledged as one of the great place names of microbiology in the United Kingdom.

New Threats and Hazards 1980–1991

From 1976 until the late 1980s CDE was considerably involved in the Yellow Rain saga, which arose from claims of the use of chemical or biological warfare against the H'Mong tribes in Laos and in Kampuchea and specifically that certain mycotoxins (fungal toxins) known as trichothecene toxins were the agents involved. The United States had, on the basis of early impressions, openly accused the USSR of a breach of the 1925 Geneva Protocol and of the Biological Weapons Convention of 1972, in supplying the agent of Yellow Rain for hostile purposes in Laos and Kampuchea. Many environmental samples from reported attacks were analysed at the Establishment The symptomatology and clinical histories of victims were studied, as was the available information on the effects of trichothecenes on man arising in certain natural disease. Trichothecenes were also produced in small quantifies from the Fusaria species of fungi and the various types extracted and identified for detailed study of their toxicology. Whilst analysis of samples at the Establishment proved negative, the epidemiological

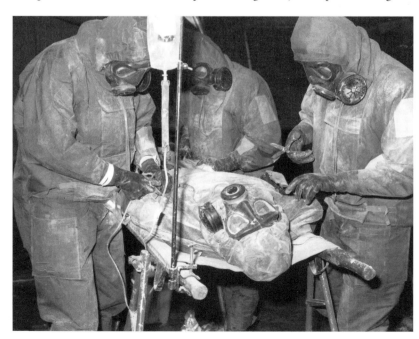

A tented chemical decontamination centre during a demonstration by a Field Ambulance and a Field Hospital of the RAMC.
This is an important stage in the evacuation of battlefield casualties, between the Regimental Aid Post and the Field Hospital. Here RAMC personnel are removing the casualty's NBC suit after its decontamination with fullers earth.

evidence led to the view that chemical attacks had occurred, albeit that the agent or agents remained unidentified and the distinctive residues of Yellow Rain were found to be bee faeces. By the late 1980s Yellow Rain attacks were almost unheard of.

However, from 1980–1982 there was reported use of chemical weapons by the USSR in Afghanistan followed by undisputed reports of the use of mustard gas and nerve agents by Iraq against Iran from 1983 and against the Kurdish element in Iraq, notably the Infamous Halabja attack in 1988 and subsequent intensive use in offensive operations against Iran. The 1979 Sverdlovsk incident had aroused concern about the USSR's compliance with the Biological Weapons Convention. This, Yellow Rain and Afghanistan all combined to engender unease about the apparently broadening global threat.

Decontamination trials aboard ship 1981.

As events subsequently showed, there were good reasons for unease. In 1992, twenty years after the former USSR had signed and ratified the Biological Weapons Convention, for which it had been, with the United Kingdom and the USA, a co-depository nation, President Yeltsin admitted that the former USSR had illegally intensified its offensive BW programme to massive proportions. The defectors, Pasechnik and Alibekov, subsequently provided detailed information on the clandestine BW programme. Ostensibly, the Russian government has denied that the programme still continues but there are many unanswered questions relating to retention of the world's largest BW programme. A 1992 presidential decree purported to ensure that Russia would fulfil its international obligations but uncertainty remains. Iraq's use of CW against Iran and the Iraqi Kurdish population from 1981–1988 is confirmed. The United Nations Special Commission's (UNSCOM) investigations in Iraq from 1991 revealed alarming data about that nation's capabilities in CW and BW. The Chemical Weapons Convention which entered into force in April 1997 has undoubtedly been effective in many respects, having an effective verification scheme but the Biological Weapons Convention which entered into force in 1975 has, as yet, no verification or enforcement provisions. The Organisation for the Prohibition of Chemical Weapons (OPCW) in The Hague was set up by the United nations to implement the CWC by inspection and verification regimes. Proliferation of CW and BW capability is increasing. The number of countries with a CW or BW capability is now probably more than ten.

In 1983, when Dr Watson left to become Director of the Building Research Establishment Dr Alan Bebbington, formerly Deputy Director (Chemistry) at CDE, was appointed Acting

USSR officers visiting Porton during the Second World War. Seated with the Russians are Air Commodore Combe the Chief Superintendent and Brigadier R M A Welchman. In the back row are (left to right) O G Sutton, Lieutenant Colonel A E Kent, Edgar Bateman, Captain D C Evans and an unidentified officer.

Director. After a short spell in the USA at the start of his career, Dr Bebbington came to the then Chemistry Research Section at Porton in 1953 and became Superintendent of the Chemistry Division in 1972. In June 1984 Dr G S Pearson, previously Director General (Research and Development) in the Royal Ordnance Factories, was appointed Director of CDE.

The 1980s were marked by the re-appraisal of the biological threat, the assessment that recombinant-DNA techniques and biotechnology might be misused to obtain a massive advancement in its biological warfare potential by any nation which possessed or intended to possess such capabilities. Chemical and biological weapons were no longer fairly well separated methods of war; their agents now formed a continuous spectrum. Hand-in-hand with these newer hazards was the spectre of proliferation.

The USSR stated unequivocally for the first time in 1987 that it possessed chemical weapons and provided details to the international community during the negotiations for a Chemical Weapons Convention. In 1988, as part of confidence-building moves connected with the proposed Convention, a party from the USSR chemical warfare facility at Shikhany and other departments visited CDE for a week of visits and discussions. At the end of June in the same year there was a reciprocal visit to Shikhany by a British team which included CDE staff. On both occasions the United Kingdom teams were jointly led by the Director of CDE and the United Kingdom Ambassador to the Conference on Disarmament in Geneva. Greater openness on these matters between the USSR

At Shikhany; June 1988. British scientists from Porton with representatives from other Ministry of Defence Departments and the Foreign and Commonwealth Office made an historic visit to the USSR chemical warfare facility at Shikhany. Earlier in June, USSR representatives came to Porton. The only previous official USSR visit had been during the Second World War when the Red Army Officers visited Porton.

and the West and the increasingly detailed negotiations for a verifiable and effective Chemical Weapons Convention were balanced by reported Libyan production of chemical agents at Rabta and intimations of even more proliferation occurring in many parts of the world.

However, whatever the hazards in future military conflicts, the United Kingdom forces are probably still the best equipped in the world for chemical and biological defence. The newest S10 respirator, the No 1 NBC suit Mark IV and the array of sophisticated detection and monitoring equipment available in-service or under development are unsurpassed. Training in chemical defence by the Army was considerably enhanced by the creation in 1979 of the Porton Battle Run on the ranges. This unique facility enables visiting units to deploy realistically for 36–48 hours over many miles of the range with differing topography. The unit is exposed to realistic attack with agent simulants from the ground or air and can enact drills and adopt the full protective ensemble and practice decontamination. Their performance can be readily assessed. The Battle Run is managed and staffed by the Sector and is utilised for training by United Kingdom army units. The chemical and biological defence readiness of the British Forces was exemplified in the Gulf following the Iraqi invasion of Kuwait in August 1990. Fortunately, the Iraqi chemical and biological capabilities were not used against the coalition forces; there can be no doubt that the

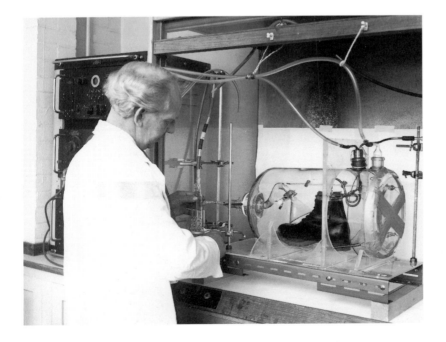

Measuring the penetration of a chemical warfare agent through an army boot. Protection of the feet is especially important as the hazard from contaminated ground may, with certain agents, persist for many days after an attack.

The May 1988 visit by USSR military scientists and diplomats.

high level of United Kingdom defence preparedness must have been a major factor influencing the Iraqi decision. Whilst the use of chemical agents against well protected forces was not likely to have been effective, as it had been against the relatively poorly protected Iranians or the unprotected Kurds, the hazards likely to be encountered by United Kingdom Forces were considerable. Further, our Forces had not been exposed to any such hazard since 1918.

Operation GRANBY: The Gulf Hostilities and Operational Support: 1990–1991

A British soldier in the Gulf drinks from his water bottle through a special tube built into his respirator.

The Iraqi invasion of Kuwait and its subsequent failure to withdraw by the 15 January 1991 deadline imposed by the United Nations Security Council Resolution 678, projected the Establishment into active operational support of United Kingdom forces in the Gulf. The Establishment devoted considerable resources which involved two-thirds of the senior staff for part of the time: this equated to the full time effort of a third of the staff; much other activity was necessarily curtailed. Contributions were made to of the intelligence communities assessment of the threat, notably on characteristics of agents, the implications for British operations, the consequences of Iraqi deployment of ballistic missiles with chemical or biological warheads and likely scenarios for their use. The hazard distances which could arise from Allied conventional weapon attacks on Iraqi chemical and biological facilities were assessed; as were those which could arise from

PATRIOT interception of SCUD-type missiles with chemical or biological warheads. Estimates were provided on the persistency of agents in the climatic conditions which existed in the Gulf. A considerable effort was devoted to an analysis of the likely effects of Iraqi chemical and biological attacks on Allied Forces at several fixed sites and in mobile operation states. Urgent and successful measures were taken to augment the already in-service chemical agent detectors and monitoring devices and an interim system for the detection of biological agent aerosols was designed, developed and dispatched to the Gulf, together with Service operators trained at the Establishment For confirmation of such attacks and highly specific identification of the agents, a system for collection of samples was devised, trialled, produced and deployed, together with trained Service personnel within three months.

Advice was constantly sought by and given to the Ministry of Defence, other Government departments, defence contractors, industry and individuals on the implications of chemical and biological attacks by Iraq in Gulf conditions. Much advice was provided to the Service on decontamination topics and the agent persistency that might be expected in the climate and conditions of the Gulf. Most Western nations data on such matters had, of course, arisen from work which related largely to the more temperate conditions of a war in Europe. In extremely hot conditions certain chemical agents may present quite different and often greatly enhanced hazards. The potency of mustard gas may be

The British troops in the Gulf war were the most well equipped for defence against chemical and biological agents. Clanging mess time together was a useful means of local alarm.

increased almost two-fold with more rapid and complete vaporisation and the increased susceptibility of sweaty skin to penetration.

On the medical countermeasures, studies were done and advice provided on control of infection in wounds and the management of wounds contaminated with chemical agent. The lesions produced in the skin by mustard gas are notoriously slow to heal; the Establishment devised a surgical technique to enhance the healing rate. Casualty monitoring was implemented in conjunction with the Department of Health, the National Health Service and the Armed Forces Medical Services, to provide advice on the medical management of any chemical and biological casualties in the Gulf and at British military and civilian hospitals.

The ability of the Establishment to respond so successfully to wide-ranging problems was dependent on the existence of multi-disciplinary teams of civilian and military personnel, backed by efficient trials, engineering and administration staff; a reflection of the tradition laid down at Porton after the Great War of 1914–1918 and continued thereafter. The magnitude of the Gulf-orientated activity at Porton is shown by numerous individual Establishment reports during 1991. These also identify topics that may require further consideration and work. Acknowledgement of the Establishment's role in the Gulf War was both widespread and at the highest level. The ability to act, as well as advise, within a short time scale was particularly appreciated. In recognition of their exceptional contributions to the Establishment's support of Operation GRANBY, Dr R J Powell was awarded the CBE, Dr G J

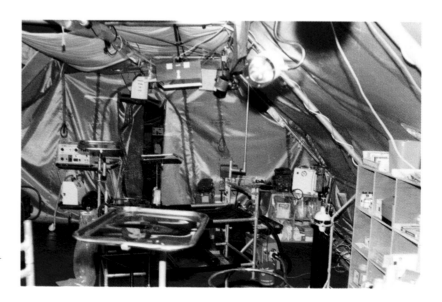

In the Gulf War this tented medical treatment facility makes use of the Porton liner concept of ensuring the gas-proofing of RAMC field hospitals and casualty clearing centres.

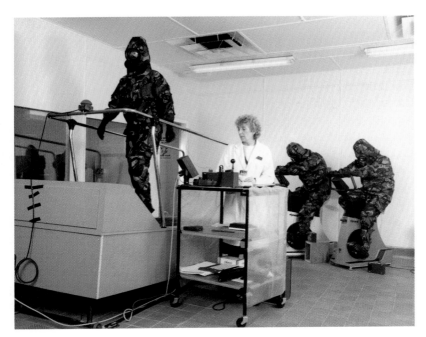

Evaluating the physiological burden of personal protection.
The protection of the body from chemical and biological warfare agents has to be developed with care. All effective protective clothing and respiratory protection can reduce fighting efficiency to a degree and the aim is to achieve maximum protection with a minimum physiological burden to the wearer. Hence the classical methods of human physiology, such as the treadmill seen here, are used to measure effects on breathing rates, body temperature and the circulation.

Cooper, Mr J W Tindle and Lieutenant Colonel H D H Keatinge were awarded the OBE and Corporal M G Lee-Bennet, the BEM. A further eleven members of staff received letters of commendation from the Under Secretary of State for Defence Procurement.

After the cease-fire, the Establishment continued to support activity relating to the United Nations Special Commission (UNSCOM) set up to oversee the destruction of Iraqi nuclear, chemical and biological weapons and of ballistic missiles. Professor Bryan Barrass OBE, as the then Superintendent of the Chemistry and Decontamination Division was appointed as the sole United Kingdom member of the Special Commission set up by the United Nations Security Council resolution 687. Subsequently Professor Barrass and several other Establishment staff visited facilities in Iraq in the course of the Commission's work up to 1999, when Iraq withdrew cooperation.

The Advent Of DERA

By 1991 CDE had become CBDE and was one of the six Defence Support Agencies under MOD's Deputy Chief Scientific Advisor, and its former Director General had been appointed its Chief Executive.

In 1995, CBDE became a part of DERA, the Defence Evaluation and Research Agency, an executive agency of MOD, evolved in 1994 from proposals of the "Front Line First" Defence Cost Studies which recommended the creation of this agency from the existing Defence Research Agency (DRA) which had been created in 1991 by the bringing together of the Royal Aerospace Establishment (RAE), the Royal Armament Research and Development Establishment (RARDE), the Royal Signals and Radar Establishment (RARDE) and the several Admiralty Establishments, by the incorporation of further MOD directorates, centres and establishments. In 1995 CBDE became a sector of DERA, with the eventual title of the CBD Sector. At first, CBDE was incorporated in a Protection and Life Sciences Division of DERA but revisions soon became evident and the CBD Sector became slightly more autonomous and now incorporates an Environmental Sciences Department based at Haslar, Winfrith and Bridgwater, all relics of onetime MOD Establishments.

Inevitably, the incorporation of CBDE within DERA led to a great deal of organisational and management change. DERA now faces the prospect of Public-Private-Partnership (PPP) but it is, as yet, not certain at the time of proofreading (2000) whether the CBD Sector will follow this route or revert to the MOD.

The Chemical and Biological Defence Establishment achieved Defence Support Agency status in April 1991, with the Director General as its Chief Executive, under the "ownership" of Dr G G Pope, MOD's Deputy Chief Scientific Advisor, who was also responsible for five other such agencies. Soon more such

The urgent needs for effective defences in the Gulf led to the rapid development of additional equipment and the instruction of servicemen in its deployment.
Here monitoring the environment by continual air sampling and subsequent analysis is being practised on the range.

agencies appeared. A CBDE Council was set up to assist the "owner" on strategic issues. The Chemical and Biological Defence Board and its Committees continued, under the aegis of the Defence Scientific Advisory Council, to provide independent scientific advice. Life at Porton appeared to have stabilised but morale was somewhat diminished by the appearance of market testing and the implications for privatisation, contractorisation or remaining in Government. In 1994 the DSAC disbanded the CBDB (and all its other Boards) and to create a new broad structure in which chemical and biological defence would be addressed by the new Chemical, Biological and Human Technologies Board. In the same year it seemed likely that CBDE had established its credibility as an Agency and the prospects of its inclusion in a new Defence Science and Technology Agency appeared. With the approaching move to MOD London and then retirement of Graham Pearson, Dr Graham Coley, then Assistant Chief Scientific Advisor (Projects) in MOD was appointed Managing Director (Designate) for CBD in 1994 when it was announced that CBDE would become part of DERA, initially as part of the short-lived Protection and Life-Sciences Division and eventually as the Chemical and Biological Defence Sector. In 1995 Graham Pearson left CBDE for MOD as Assistant Chief Scientific Advisor (Non-proliferation) and Graham Coley appeared at Porton. Later Dr Coley moved to DERA headquarters at Farnborough and Dr David Anderson became Sector Director with Dr Rick Hall as Technical Director CBDE. On 4 August 1997, Paul Taylor, who had been Superintendent of Assessment Division, was appointed Sector Director.

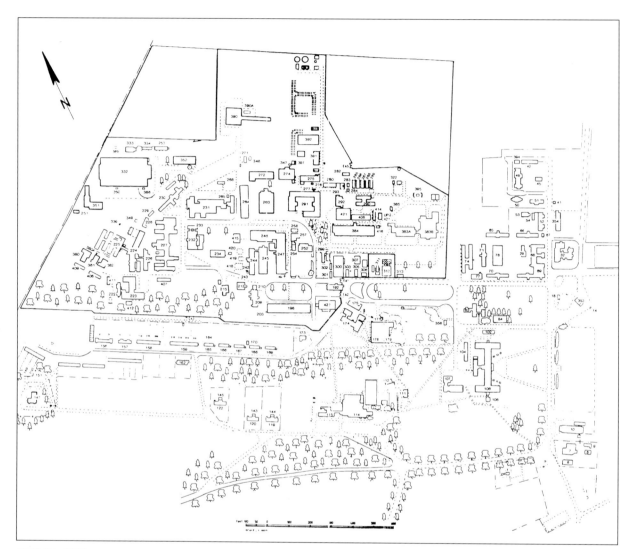

CBDE in 1992
Comparison with the aerial views and
plans of earlier years shows that many
huts and minor buildings have been
removed, as have most of the married
officers' quarters. The "Closed Area" has
changed its outline to include a new car
park and the Establishment has been
considerably enhanced by now mature
trees and shrubs.

The early years of the CBD Sector in DERA were confusing to most people at Porton: flux prevailed. Ultimately, by 1999 the CBD Sector consisted of three major departments:

Biomedical Sciences
CB (Chemical and Biological) Systems
Pan Sector Projects

Each Department has a Departmental Manager and a Technical Manager. Each Department consists of Business Groups under a Business Group Manager, supported by Team Leaders, Laboratory or Workshop Managers, Facility Managers, Building Officers, Bid Managers and Project Managers. The CBD Sector, like all of DERA, operates on a trading fund basis. All work for external customers is run as projects ie "a planned set of activities with defined start and end points, intended to achieve defined objectives". Customers are the organisations who are paying for the work. MOD is the prime customer and tasks the Sector to carry out research through the Applied Research Programme or the Corporate Research Programme. At present, income from non-MOD customers is about 15% of the total. Such customers include other UK government departments, foreign governments and outside industry. The current Business Groups include Biology, Biophysics, Microbiology, Patho-biology, Detection, Environ-

Field trials with helicopter-mounted chemical agent detectors in the 1980s on the Porton Range.

The safe disposal of old chemical munitions is one of CBDEs roles. This apparatus for opening artillery shells has recently been superseded by a remotely-controlled system. The chemical agent charging from such munitions is destroyed by burning.

mental Sciences (presently located at Haslar, Bridgwater and Winfrith), Chemistry and Hazard Assessment, Protection and Decontamination, Testing and Project Services, Assessment and Operations, Demilitarisation, Range, Incinerator and Farm, Engineering and the Management Cell.

The Anniversary Dinner

On 30 October 1991, the 75th Anniversary Dinner was held in the Main Conference Room of the Main Block at the then CBDE. The chief guests were Field Marshall Sir Richard Vincent, then Chief of the Defence Staff and Sir Michael Quinlan, the MOD's Permanent Under Secretary, together with about forty other senior representatives of all the echelons of the Services with past and present links with Porton Down, the local MP, local community leaders, the Bishop of Ramsbury, several former Directors and some twenty senior staff of the Establishment. This was probably the first dinner held at Porton Down since the closure of the Officers Mess in 1979. The old Mess silver and a quintet from the band of Her Majesty's Royal Marines, Commander-in-Chief Fleet, added lustre to this unique occasion.

Agriculture at Porton Down

Farming at Porton began during the Great War: one of the earliest sugar beet crops was produced and corn, roots and hay were produced as fodder for experimental animals. The area now farmed by the Sector, as opposed to that farmed by tenant farmers from Figsbury Rings along the A30 and A343 roads to the area known as Palestine, is largely in the vicinity of CAMR and the main Sector buildings and also extends along the Salisbury to London railway line as far as the Palestine area to include 1130 acres. The Farm and the tenanted farmland provides a physical buffer between the area of the Range available for field trials and the Porton boundary. It provides good financial returns and has an undoubted public relations function in that visitors and the public can see, peripherally, crops and farm animals thriving in an area perceived by some as having sinister connotations. To a degree, the Farm supports the trials programme by providing large animals such as pigs and sheep. The Farm helps the overall conservation plan; for many years it has liaised with the Royal Society for the Preservation of Birds to provide nesting sites for the Stone Curlew population. Of the 1130 acres, 780 acres are arable crops, 300 acres are grass and 47 acres are woodland. The arable crops are wheat and barley, linseed, peas and oilseed rape. Except for barley and wheat fed to the Sector's livestock, all produce is sold locally. Currently, there are 520 ewes that lamb outside in May to produce 800–900 lambs that will be sold commercially for meat from October to February. Steer calves are bought every May and fattened and sold for meat when 21–34 months old. All these sheep and cattle are fed home-grown products. A small herd of large white pigs is kept to provide weaners for trials; any surplus is sold. In 1992 a field of low fertility and difficult terrain was planted with hardwood trees under the Farm Woodland Premium Scheme to provide quality timber for felling in 80–100 years time. The current full-time farm staff is three, including the Farm Manager. A self-employed contract shepherd helps at lambing and other busy times. Local agricultural contractors are used for jobs such as baling, silage making, dung spreading and hedging.

The Porton Down Science Park

The south of Wiltshire has world-class scientific facilities and expertise. Much of this is within the DERA facilities at Porton Down and at Boscombe Down. Much is under the aegis of the Department of Health's facility, the Centre for Applied Microbiology and Research at Porton, the Salisbury District Council, the Wiltshire County Council, the Swindon and Wiltshire Training and Enterprise Council and the South West Regional Development Agency.

The Porton Down Science Park emerged in October 1997 as a brainchild of DERA Porton Down and was envisaged as fulfilling the government policies of defence diversification and economic competitiveness by exploiting the facilities and expertise already existing in Wiltshire and to generate United Kingdom wealth and prestige. The major capital investment within the Sector now nearing completion will help to maintain this position well into the next century. The Science Park provides a business infrastructure which allows civil companies to benefit from the Sector's facilities and research through a cluster of military and civil organisations with a common purpose on the Porton Down site to foster technology transfer and collaboration. The fields of relevance include:

  environmental engineering and modelling
  biotechnology
  healthcare
  analysis and detection systems
  instrument development
  materials technology and testing
  colloid science
  drug evaluation
  vaccine development

The facilities at DERA Porton Down, DERA Boscombe Down and CAMR will enable businesses to draw upon their expertise and resources. Suitable premises will be provided for both start-up firms and established businesses within the Park, resulting in a biomedical and biotechnological cluster around the nucleus of expertise already present on site.

There are three facets to the park. Firstly, the recycling and re-use of existing buildings. Already, 1000²m of office and laboratory accommodation now 70% occupied by tenants exist within the former Officers Mess. As the capital investment increases a further 30002m of units will be released.

Secondly, the re-development of "brown field" sites. Already about 3 hectares are available and a further 10 hectares are contemplated. Thirdly, an area of 10 hectares has been identified for new building, with the support of the District and County Councils. The advantages for DERA and the incoming civil industries are massive. The socio-economic benefits for the area are self-evident. The Science Park will provide a premier health care-environmental-aerospace cluster for Wiltshire. There will be new jobs, new businesses, the relocation of private sector companies to the area and the prospect of the Science Park emerging as a leading internationally-acknowledge centre. Already, the Science Park has three tenants and another seven are in the pipeline. The Science Park is one of the most exciting concepts in the future expansion of DERA at Porton Down.

Opprobrium

6

Without extensive research in newspaper libraries it is difficult to determine when parliamentary, media and public concern about activities at Porton Down started. It was certainly evident in the early 1920s when the British Union for the Abolition of Vivisection and the National Anti-Vivisection Society's concern centered around the use of experimental animals. Others were anxious about the legitimacy of chemical warfare and the United Kingdom's policy on this matter. In the 1930s, concern about the availability of respirators and the degree of protection afforded by them for the civilian population became increasingly prominent. In November and December of 1930 Parliamentary Questions and Enquiries on animal use were raised every week. Parliamentary questions about the exposure of volunteers to poison gases at Porton probably first arose in 1930, when it was stated that in 1929, 524 volunteer Servicemen had been exposed, including 293 volunteers from units outside the Station. The latter were largely from the Army Gas School at Winterbourne Gunner. At this time, as during the Great War, it was the custom for Servicemen of the Station to volunteer for experimental work and field trials which involved unprotected or partially protected exposure to chemical war agents eg with the "object of testing the penetration of respirators or in testing the effect of some new gas on the human subject for the Physiology Department". Crossley, the first Commandant, in his 1919 report on Porton in the Great War, pays tribute to the officers, NCOs and men of the Station "who suffered pain and discomfort so readily and cheerfully". By 1922 the Physiological Sub-Committee of the Chemical Warfare Committee observed that the repeated use of volunteers from the Station's military personnel was in danger of evoking some hypersensitivity or even general debility and recommended that steps should be taken to relieve Porton's own personnel from this voluntary duty. Appeals to neighbouring units for assistance met with little response and in the hope of attracting outside volunteers, the Commandant suggested that "danger money" be paid to men volunteering for tests. Whilst this proposal received sympathetic consideration from the War Office, it is doubtful whether any financial inducement was offered at that time. In 1924 provision was made for "medical leave" for men who might experience "excessive discomfort during tests". Volunteer recruitment was put on a more official basis in 1925 when the War

Office argued that volunteers could be sought within Southern Command, Subsequently, this was extended to Western and Scottish Command and arrangements were made for six Service volunteers to appear each fortnight. By 1930 regulations appeared for non-commissioned volunteers to be paid 1/- per test for "gas tests" and 6d per test for those not involving discomfort, with an additional incentive of seven days leave for every ten tests. In 1931 the Royal Navy and Royal Air Force began to produce volunteers and by 1932 the system was producing six men each week. At that time, the financial rewards appear to have lapsed, although a day's leave was given for each test completed. By 1934 a more formalised system existed and arrangements were being made for six months ahead. Soon after, the Royal Navy and Royal Air Force were unable to provide their quotas and the Army sustained the system until 1936 when the other Services re-assumed their commitments, although by then staff cuts at Porton had reduced the need for volunteers. By March 1937 sixteen men each week were needed and irregularity of supply caused complaints. In 1938 and 1939 attempts were made to meet the target, without great success. Porton's 1941 proposal to pay 2/6d to men receiving mustard gas burns was rejected by the War Office because of possible legal complications; extra leave remained the only benefit for Service volunteers. Then a local decision to pay men the shilling a test recorded ten years earlier. The War Office then decided that this scale of payment was excessive and it was limited to between 10/- and 15/- for a week's work. It was also decided that in wartime extra leave could not be considered. Matters improved slowly during the Second World War but the system remained virtually unchanged until 1950 when the urgency of the nerve agent programme required 10–20 men each week. In 1956 authority was given to increase payment to 2/- a test. Between 1959 and 1962 volunteer numbers decreased, the 20 men each week target was rarely reached. During the 1960s a considerable public relations scheme was instituted to attract volunteers, including a Services Kinema Corporation film on the volunteer programme; this had but a short-term effect. Deficiencies continue at the present time, due to manpower shortage and the increased commitments of the Services.

For nearly a decade there has been no exposure of volunteers to any chemical warfare agents, however small the quantity. Largely, the Sector has all the data needed in this field. Therapeutic or prophylactic drugs may still be administered to volunteers but only after comprehensive animal tests and after the agreement of an Independent Ethics Committee, created in 1991 to provide totally independent control over human experimentation and conformity with the Helsinki Declaration of 1961 and the Royal College of Physicians guidelines drawn up in the 1980s. Some human studies, largely concerned with respirators and other individual protective equipment continue. Volunteers, whether Service or occasionally Sector staff, receive financial rewards based on the number of tests they have undergone. In 1998 the payment was £1.97 per test, which may be based upon an injection, the giving of a blood sample or participating in some essentially physiological or psychological test. The average Service volunteer coming to the Sector for a two week period may receive £200–400 before tax in payment. All volunteers are fully briefed on the nature of the investigation in which they participate and sign their voluntary consent. All may withdraw at any time without adverse comment or penalty. Service volunteers are housed during their stay in modern accommodation of the highest standard.

The utility of the Service Volunteer Scheme at Porton over the years has been immense. It has, of course, been the subject of media, public and parliamentary concern, almost since its inception. Much of this has been misplaced and it has to be said that the majority of Service volunteers have come and gone and are none the worse for their attendance. Trials with volunteers have always been carried out with the utmost regard for the safety, health and well-being of the volunteers but on 6 May 1953 there was a sad and unfortunate incident when Leading Aircraftsman Ronald Maddison of the RAF died at the then CDEE after a test. He was one of a group of six Service volunteers participating in a test within a 100m^3 gas chamber which had already been carried out on 254 men to determine the degree of blood cholinesterase inhibition produced by the percutaneous deposition of the nerve agent Sarin (known also as GB) on the bare skin or, as in Maddison's case, through two layers of clothing (ordinary flannel Army shirting and Battle Dress serge) worn as a large patch on the forearm. All the volunteers were protected from nerve agent vapour by respirators. The liquid nerve agent was applied as twenty measured drops, each containing 10 milligrams, to the outer surface of the top layer of fabric by a calibrated pipette. The total dose was 200 milligrams, a dose which had earlier been applied to 70 other volunteers without lasting ill effects. Blood samples (for determination of the enzyme cholinesterase level) had been taken earlier: if the level of cholinesterase in the blood had been low, the volunteer would not have been used. A blood sample was also taken a few hours before the test and would have been taken soon after the test, to see the extent of any lowering of cholinesterase. Some little time after the administration of nerve agent, Ronald Maddison indicated to the CDEE staff in the chamber, that he did not feel well. He was immediately taken out of the chamber, the fabric patch and his respirator removed and he was taken by ambulance to the Station Hospital accompanied by the RAMC medical officer who had been observing the tests through the chamber windows and who had already administered the antidote atropine. Despite prolonged attention by four medical men, he died. An autopsy at the Salisbury General Infirmary found that "the appearances were compatible with those which would be found by over-action of the parasympathetic nervous system or by reduction of cholinesterase". A subsequent Court of Enquiry was held at CDEE on 11–12 May and continued in London on 28 May 1953. This confirmed inter alia that death was due to GB and must be attributed to personal idiosyncrasy which "may be related to the physiology of his skin which had allowed an unusually rapid absorption of the material or to his having an unusual sensitivity to the effects of the nerve gas that has absorbed, or the combination of both factors". The Coroners Inquest, held in camera on the instructions of the Home Office, concluded that his death was due to misadventure. There was considerable secrecy surrounding the death, the inquest, the official enquiry and the report of a special committee chaired by Dr E D Adrian (later the first Lord Adrian) of the Chemical Defence Advisory Board's Biology Committee set up under the aegis of the MOS Advisory Council on Scientific Research and Technical Development. This secrecy had its roots in preventing public knowledge of the extent of UK interest in the nerve agents and that human volunteers were being used in nerve agent studies. Links between nerve agents and Porton Down were probably first suggested in the media in 1952. Links between nerve agents and the Maddison death identified by Chapman Pincher first appeared in the press on 2 November 1953. The secrecy at the time of the fatality is understandable: it appeared to be founded on the principle that no indication of the extent of UK interest in nerve agents should be exposed. The topic, curiously is re-discovered at intervals by the media or researchers in the Public Record Office and presented to the public as a recently discovered gem from the perfidious history of Porton. A fairly full (if inaccurate) report appeared in Harris and Paxman's book in 1982 and this has been reiterated in other texts, press articles and television programmes to the present day. Relevant MOS papers are in the Public Record Office. In 1999 a former volunteer Serviceman has again raised the matter and attempted to stimulate police prosecutions for corporate manslaughter and other charges against the Sector, with accusations that CDEE staff were attempting to define the lethal dose in man or "how long nerve agent took to penetrate uniform before it would kill". In this context, there have also been claims that volunteers had been duped into participating in tests at Porton in the Past, under the guise that they were volunteering for research on the common cold (the MRC Common Cold Research Unit once existed at Harvard Hospital, Salisbury, from 1946–1989 and depended on the availability of civilian volunteers for its experimental work). In recent years a past volunteer helpline has been installed in the Sector to aid in the identification of tests which could have contributed to the present medical condition of one time Service volunteers. So far the number of enquiries has been very small. Over 20,000 Servicemen and women have attended Porton Down as volunteers and only a little over 300 enquiries have ensued. Present volunteer needs are advertised to the three Services in Defence Council Instructions and more informally by presentations to units or groups at places such as the Defence Nuclear, Biological and Chemical Centre and the School of Infantry. We also rely heavily on word-of-mouth recommendations from recent Service volunteers within their units.

A DERA leaflet "Porton Down Volunteers" (and a DERA web site) provides all inquirers with what is available within the records at the Sector and how they should proceed further at Porton, within the Service medical records, the War Pensions Agency and in submitting claims against MOD. Notwithstanding the paucity of the earliest records, which may be little more than entries in laboratory notebooks, every attempt is made to fulfil inquirers enquiries about the nature of the experiments in which they were involved.

It should be remembered that quite apart from the use of volunteers at Porton, all British Servicemen had, since the 1920s, participated in anti-gas training which involved exposure to chemical warfare agents, designed to create confidence in the efficacy of protective drills and equipment.

Up to 1940 the use of real chemical warfare agents for training in Service units had been restricted to a tear gas (CAP, CN or chloracetophenone) and a nose gas (DM, Adamsite or diphenylamine chloroarsine), the latter probably now better classified as a vomiting agent. These two agents had generally been available in ampoules for use in chambers. Smelling sets containing small amounts of mustard gas, lewisite, phosgene and a teargas (BBC) were used in lectures and teargas generators were used in the open air. From 1940 a wide range of agents was used in training. Every man was exposed to nose gas at least once and the fact recorded in his pay book. Every man was to have a drop of mustard gas placed on his arm and then required to decontaminate this with anti-gas ointment to demonstrate that early decontamination would nullify effects. Phosgene was also available in cylinders for outdoor use. By 1941 gas compounds were available widely in all commands in the United Kingdom. The compound enclosed a gas chamber where nose gases and teargases could be demonstrated, a concrete surface where mustard gas could be used and a selection of typical terrains where mustard gas simulants could be placed to show what this gas looked like on a variety of surfaces. By 1942 exercises were introduced where contaminated weapons were decontaminated, contaminated ground was traversed and effective respirator protection against mustard gas vapour was demonstrated by exposure for up to 30 minutes. All ranks in the three Services throughout the UK and the Dominions, including the Women's Services, notionally underwent this type of training without ill effect. This method of training paid a high dividend and did much to banish an untoward fear of gas and confirm the efficacy of anti-gas drills. With the nerve agents it was not possible, because of their very high toxicity, to use them in troop training. Later, doubts about the ethical aspects of exposing man to mutagenic or carcinogenic compounds led to withdrawal of mustard gas for troop training. At the present, the only agent used in this way is the essentially anti-riot control agent CS, although several simulants eg methyl salicylate (oil of wintergreen) may still be used in a limited way for "contaminating" equipment but not for direct application to the body. By 1943 the Army Council (and presumably the analogous bodies for the other Services) had laid down that all ranks must qualify in the tests for elementary anti-gas drills before being entitled to proficiency pay.

Thus, it is a fact not generally recognised that most British Servicemen and women during the pre-war decade, the Second World War and the two decades following, received minimal exposure to some sort of chemical warfare agent. The nerve agents were, of course, never used for such purposes and the exposure of British Servicemen to these was limited to the volunteers who attended at Porton Down from 1945. The past history of the Porton volunteer scheme is at present under investigation by the Wiltshire Constabulary, stimulated by information provided to the police by some past volunteers, who are alleging that some activities were illegal. The investigation, authorised by the Crown Prosecution Service, is said to lead to possible charges of corporate man-slaughter in the case of Ronald Maddison and the administration of noxious substances and assault. The CBD Sector is collaborating fully with the police in this matter.

It would be impossible to even merely list here the aspects of the past and present CBD Sector activity which have attracted opprobrium. Some are old concerns, often re-discovered or re-vitalised at intervals over the decades. These include the belief that the former CDEE/CDE and MRE continued, despite the Government's 1956 decision to abandon offensive chemical and biological warfare, to sustain almost clandestinely preparations for such weapon development. Happily, such accusations have disappeared in recent years but there is still little public awareness of the 1956 change in policy, and the constraints imposed by the Chemical Weapons convention of 1993, the Chemical Weapons Act of 1996, the Biological and Toxin Weapons Convention of 1972 and the Biological Weapons Act of 1974. Equally, there seems to be little awareness of the major part played by the United Kingdom in the protracted negotiations for the 1972 and the 1996 Conventions.

The principal manifestations of the former chemical warfare capability have all gone. The plants at Sutton Oak and Nancekuke no longer exist, the Second World War Agency Factories have been destroyed or converted to civil chemical production and the wartime stockpiles of bulk agents and charged munitions are all destroyed. However, there is a minuscule residue of usually buried chemical warfare munitions formerly held by Service units which crop up occasionally and evoke local concern. Some of these may be of the Great War period or from the 1930s, others may be of Second World War origin. Suspect chemical munitions and troop-training aids unearthed by Explosive Ordnance Disposal units are brought to the Sector for examination, emptying and the safe incineration of the chemical charging. Also, decontamination of the burial sites may be arranged. Probably the most recent major exercise of this sort was the survey of fields near the Defence NBC Centre at Winterbourne Gunner near Salisbury in 1999, when 49 Field Squadron of the Royal Engineers located over 800 pieces of buried munitions on a Great War mortar range in the one million pound Operation ABBOT. The media had increased local anxiety about the safety of the land, particularly that backing onto household gardens. In the event, very few of the buried items were chemical weapons although some smoke devices and a number of glass tubes containing chemical warfare agents dating from the Great War were discovered in a buried rubbish dump on the MOD land. The Sector has special expertise in incinerating agents removed from munitions and it is capable of incinerating 2 tonnes of material each day under the most safe conditions. Generally, as far as buried chemical munitions are concerned, most are of the 1914–1918 period. Inevitably, historical records of military land usage are fairly superficial. After the Great War there was a tendency to bury or sea-dump chemical munitions rather than return them to depots for large scale destruction of the agent, as was generally done in the 1950s–1960s when the United Kingdom's stockpile was destroyed. In February 1999, three buried Livens containers were discovered at Hythe and transferred to Porton Down for evaluation and destruction. As the natural source of any domestic problem, real or imagined, concerned with chemical and biological warfare in the United Kingdom, Porton Down will inevitably be linked in some way, identified as some sort of culprit. The deep-sea dumping of unwanted chemical munitions after the Second World War provides an almost continuous source of largely political concern. The United Kingdom disposal of 116,000 tons of German chemical munitions in the Skagerrak and 120,000 tons of its own by loading into hulks which were then scuttled in the Atlantic. All the major belligerents of the Second World War dumped chemical munitions at sea. Detailed records of all such United Kingdom dumpings were undoubtedly made but after the disposal of munitions, there seemed to be no good reason to retain such records indefinitely and with the passage of time most were destroyed; no reason was seen at the time for their retention. However, contemporary media curiosity shows that such destruction of records was premature. The media often claims the existence of cover-ups and a reticence to provide information but there was no policy of deliberate record destruction in the United Kingdom and most former sea-dumping nations have the same deficits in their knowledge. Where there are data, relevant reports have been compiled and provided to international bodies: a very full MOD report was handed to the 1993 Helsinki Commission enquiry into chemical munitions dumped in the Baltic. The United Kingdom's 1945 storage of 71,000 German nerve agent bombs at RAF Llandwrog and their 1956–1957 sea dumping in the Atlantic Ocean in Operation SANDCASTLE has attracted parliamentary and media coverage for decades, despite fairly precise information being provided by MOD in 1970 and reported in the press. A good and almost definitive account of this lengthy drama was given by the Welsh author Roy Sloan in his 1998 book but it is unlikely to inhibit media re-discovery and sensationalisation in the future.

The chemical weapon trials conducted by CDEE at Obanakoro in Nigeria during 1951–1955 have also attracted undue attention since 1982, when they were first publicised in Harris and Paxman's book and later in Thomas's 1985 book. The essential need was to evaluate the effect of realistic nerve agent dissemination from munitions in a hot and wet climate. This was done by trials teams from CDEE using munitions charged by hand at Porton with the nerve agent GB. Authors have inferred that this trialling in tropical conditions reflected a considerable development of United Kingdom nerve agent munitions; it did not. There was no stockpile from which nerve agent munitions could be drawn. There was further concern that contaminated trials sites remained in Nigeria; they did not, since GB is not a persistent agent on terrain.

The 1942 and 1943 trials conducted by Biology Department, Porton, on Gruinard Island were a different kettle of fish. They subsequently provided a source of concern for over forty years. Here bomb trials with spores of Bacillus anthracis resulted in contamination of island terrain for nearly 50 years. Years of parliamentary and public concern were exacerbated by the media. This was not helped by the need for secrecy about the nature of the contamination which precluded de-requisition and the return of the island to its owner after the end of the war: the owner could not be told the nature of the contamination. Equally, there was uncertainty that the matter could be resolved. This resulted in the 1946 purchase of the island by the Crown, with the promise that when the contamination no longer existed, the owner or her legatees could re-purchase the island for £500. The level of anthrax spores in the soil showed no signs of diminishing and methods of decontamination of the island seemed prohibitively expensive. A team from Porton visited the island each year from 1947–1968 to take soil samples and check on the warning notices about dangerous contamination and a prohibition on landing. Sporadically, but

Gruinard Island in 1986, as seen from the mainland.
The spit of shingle seen extending from right of the island provided a convenient landing place from the mainland jetty, both for the field trials teams of 1942 and 1943, and those from Porton and contractors who decontaminated sites on the island in 1986 and 1987 in preparation for its 1990 return to civil ownership, nearly 50 years after its acquisition to meet urgent war time needs.

The decontamination of Gruinard Island in 1986.
Contractor's personnel irrigating a contaminated area with a solution of formaldehyde in sea water. About 50 litres were applied to every square metre of the ten acres so treated.

increasingly, questions were asked in Parliament and the press on why the island was being retained and what was the nature of the wartime trials which precluded its return. In 1967, after some de-classification of the Gruinard story was thought advisable, the warning signs were augmented to show the nature of the contamination. Published speculation was considerable and occasionally explicit. A public relations presence was included in the 1962 inspection to deal with the press. In 1966 a MOD press release coincided with the annual visit and confirmed that anthrax spores had been disseminated to assess the feasibility of biological warfare and to define the necessary countermeasures against possible enemy use of biological warfare during the war. This was, of course, something of an inadequate statement; the trials were to determine the feasibility of biological warfare but, this having been demonstrated by the first trial, the work was then directed towards the development of a retaliatory offensive capability by the United Kingdom. This fact was not directly apparent until about 1981 and then not from any official statement. It was not until about 1990 that any open publication revealed unequivocally the policy underlying the Gruinard Island trials.

The sad death of Geoffrey Bacon of MRE on 1 August 1962 from plague evoked considerable and prolonged media coverage. There was no doubt that the fatal infection arose from his laboratory work on Yersinia pestis, the causative bacterium. The strain of Yersinia pestis isolated from his sputum was identical with that on which he was working, in a programme using bacterial genetics and concerned with the development of a better vaccine for the disease. The event led to national newspaper headlines such as "Secret Death Riddle", "Germ War Scientist in Death Mystery", "Germ War Expert Dies", "Death Mystery at Germ War Plant", "Germ Scientist Died of Plague" etc etc and a hefty aftermath of articles such as "Safety Measures at Porton", "Plague Virus (sic) Escapes Security", "New Safety Measures To Be Enforced at Germ Warfare Centre", "More Germ Safeguards Urged". The safety aspects of the Microbiological Research Establishment were exacerbated on 28 August 1962, a near-month after the Geoffrey Bacon tragedy when an autoclave (a pressurised steam sterilising vessel) exploded, shattering two windows. This inevitably evoked a further rash of media attention with headlines such as "Blast Rocks Plague Death Station", "Explosion at Black Death Laboratory", followed by concern from county and local government authorities reported in headlines such as "More Germ Safeguards Urged", "Report By MOH at Porton: Call for Bullet Proof Windows", "Germ Secrecy Maintained: Councils in Porton Area Protest", "Excessive Secrecy at Germ Centre" and "War Office Ignores our Safety Demands".

By the mid-1960s anti-Porton demonstrations were frequent under the aegis of the Committee of 100 and other organisations. These evoked headlines such as "2000 Troops Will Face Germ Mobs", "Stop the Germ March Now", etc. In 1968 feelings were exacerbated by the BBC programme "Towards Tomorrow" film "A Plague on Your Children", which was filmed in part at Porton Down, which the Establishments had hoped would provide much-needed enlightenment of Porton's role. As "The Times" stated on 6 June 1968 "Porton Down is now displacing Aldermaston in the demonology of collective protest against the horrors of war". On 24 January 1969 a seven hour "teach-in" on chemical and biological defence was held at Edinburgh University. The speakers included Mr G D Heath, Director of Biological and Chemical Defence in MOD, Mr Neville Gadsby, Director of CDEE, Mr John Morris, Minister of Defence for Equipment, and a large number of eminent scientists and academics. The same year saw the foundation of the British Society for Social Responsibility in Science which took a largely anti-Porton stance. The MRE also came under fire in the House of Lords in February 1969 when there was a strong movement to place it under the Ministry of Health.

Throughout this period the Chemical Defence Establishment at Nancekuke was not neglected by the media or the public and was the scene of many protests marches. By 1962 it had become an integral part of the then CDEE as the Process Research Division and later the Process Chemistry Division of the CDE at Porton Down. The main preoccupation was that vast stocks of nerve gas were held at Nancekuke: this was not so.

In 1968 a week of open days was held at the MRD. The main purpose of this, and a similar week at the then CDEE in 1969, was to kill the myth that work was being secretly carried out on offensive matters and to demonstrate the spectrum of research topics involved in the evaluation of the hazards and effective means of defence. A very wide range of political figures, academics, industrialists, scientists, journalists, members of various organisations and the general public visited during these weeks and were able to enter most of the facilities within each of the two Establishments. A similar series of open days was also held at Nancekuke in 1969, to be followed by a special Press Day in 1970. On all these occasions the opportunity was taken to promulgate messages from the Minister of Defence, Mr Denis Healy, justifying the existence of the Establishments. Were the open days successful? They must have demonstrated to most visitors that fears about offensive capabilities under development at Porton and Nancekuke were unfounded. However, there were always those who chose not be convinced: inevitably, these were usually the most vociferous.

Other matters were attracting somewhat hostile concern, some internal in nature. Extra-mural research in British universities funded by Porton was perceived as loaded with sinister overtones. The products of Porton's entirely defensively-orientated research being made available to the United States (which still maintained offensive capabilities in both chemical and biological warfare and had not ratified the 1925 Geneva Protocol) was a particularly difficult problem for the United Kingdom. Few realised that the United Kingdom received massive amounts of valuable reciprocal data from the United States, whose research activities in these fields were vast and diverse. The limited United States use of non-lethal harassing chemical warfare agents such as DM, CS and CN against Viet Cong troops in Vietnam and the extensive use of defoliants exacerbated international concern about not only such use but the United Kingdom's role in collaborative research deemed to support such use. The 1969 abandonment of the United States biological weapons capability, the subsequent abandonment of its chemical warfare capability, its intention to submit the 1925 Geneva Protocol to the Senate for ratification and the intention to sign the forthcoming Biological Weapons Convention, produced some lessening of international opprobrium. The United States eventually ratified the Geneva Protocol in 1975. By that time it had destroyed its biological weapons and destruction of its chemical warfare capability was well underway.

In recent times it is perhaps the emergence into the public domain of United Kingdom activity of yesteryear that has evoked much national concern. The availability of documents in the Public Record Office about the 1953–1964 dissemination of aerosols of zinc cadmium sulphide by the then CDEE over vast tracts of England and Wales, produced much criticism. Firstly, on the grounds of secret disseminations involving exposure of the public and secondly, on the possible toxic nature of this simulant. At the time of writing, this matter is under an independent investigation by Professor Peter Lachmann FRS and a small group of similarly distinguished medical men and scientists, who will report eventually to the Minster of Defence. The dissemination of aerosols of harmless bacteria over the Dorset coast and southern counties by the MRE from 1961 until the closure of the Establishment in 1979, and of earlier work from 1941 in other areas of the United Kingdom (and at sea in the West Indies and Scottish waters) where there was al fresco dissemination of pathogens at sea eg in Operation HARNESS, evoked earlier concern. The trials on the Dorset coast were examined in 1999 by Professor Brian Spratt FRS, an independent medical man recommended, as was Professor Lachmann, by the President of the Royal Society, to advise the Minister of Defence on the possible health hazards of the large-scale dissemination of non-pathogenic bacteria over Dorset. Professor Spratt concluded that such hazards were unlikely to have existed.

These two types of field trial were not the only trials to have evoked public anger in recent years. Publicity in 1995 about trials conducted by the MRE in the 1960s which involved the dissemination of aerosols of the harmless Bacillus globigii spores with the London Underground system and thus the unwitting exposure of the public to inhaled spores was considerable.

The opprobrium which all these past activities and events attract (and only a handful have been recounted here) is often misguided. It is regrettable that the ethical and safety aspects of yesteryear continue to be viewed by the standards which prevail today. Such contemporary standards might undoubtedly preclude the type of activity allowed decades ago, particularly that which arose from the contingencies of the Second World War or the Cold War era. We should not judge the events of the past by today's standards and attitudes. It is quite clear that, in the past, activities were engaged in at Porton or by the Porton establishments which would not be countenanced today.

One matter which has been a constant feature since the Great War is the use of experimental animals in chemical and biological defence research. There is little point in embarking on a philosophical discussion of the issues here. People, in any event, operate from preconceived notions on the use of animals in research and are not likely to be diverted by rhetoric. What, however, must not be denied is that the animal use in the Sector at Porton is conducted under the terms of the Animal (Scientific Procedures) Act of 1986, the overview of the DERA Independent Animal Welfare Committee and the Home Office inspectors. Thus, the highest standards of laboratory animal care and welfare exist. In all studies, those responsible must actively consider the alternative possibilities of using cells or tissues derived from animals or man, the possibility of reducing animal numbers and the refining of experimental design to maximise information from the minimum number of animals. The Sector does not conduct animal experiments for the development or evaluation of weapons of war and will not accept non–MOD work involving animals in routine regulatory testing of cosmetics or the testing of tobacco products. The Sector's use of animals in research is less than half of one per cent of all animal experimentation carried out in the United Kingdom. The species currently bred at Porton are rhesus monkeys, common marmosets, mice, rats, sheep and pigs: others, such as rabbits and guinea pigs, are bought from suppliers licensed by the Home Office. There has been no use of dogs and cats in the last near-decade: this has always been a particularly emotive matter. These brief statements are worth recording here, irrespective of the near certainty that they will not alter the view of the objector to the use of animals in research.

No other Sector of DERA has this long history of opprobrium. It has its roots in the particularly emotive nature of chemical and biological warfare: such roots have extended into the explicitly defensive programme which has existed from the mid–1950s and continues now.

The extraordinary secrecy which attended almost any manifestation of chemical and biological warfare for decades has been removed in recent times. Some secrecy must remain on our current evaluation of threats and hazards, and on some aspects of defence but this secrecy is now essentially related to defence and not also to political sensitivity. Past secrecy has encourage contemporary unease and opprobrium but as past activity is revealed and promulgated, such opprobrium must slowly diminish. One of the objects of this book is to promulgate Porton's past, present and, to a degree, its future, and encourage opprobrium to wither. If you want

to know more, consult some of the texts listed in the two biblio-
graphies to this book: not all in the second are strictly accurate and
a few are valueless but at least these provide a basis for exploration.
Those items in the first bibliography can be regarded as authoritative, albeit that some of the earlier papers in the open literature
may have omitted some facts.

Recent Research Highlights

7

It is more than eight years since the 1992 book "Porton Down: 75 Years of Biological and Chemical Research" was written. There was, in that text, a small element of reporting some of the research which had been done in the 1980s. Some of this reporting was necessarily bland and diffuse because of the defence security restrictions which existed then. More importantly, space precluded a detailed listing of the totality of research topics: some such considerations and constraints still exist. Much of the research in the Sector is published, albeit in often specialised scientific journals and periodicals which may be almost unknown to the public. Further, there are obvious difficulties in summarising the detail of scientific publications in a way that the average reader can comprehend. Nevertheless, this section identifies and expands briefly on some of the more significant research in the Sector in the last eight years or so. The research described is essentially practical: scholarly assessments of threat, hazard, feasibility, specific defence equipment options and the future of chemical and biological warfare are not addressed here, for obvious reasons.

Trauma and Surgery

The control of microbial infection after surgery involving the use of synthetic vascular graft material is a problem for both civil and military surgeons. This and the more general problem of the control of infection in wounds has been the subject of research. The protection of Explosive Ordnance Disposal (EOD) personnel in the Services and the police has been markedly improved following research on the mechanics of bomb blast and subsequent traumatic amputation, in collaboration between the CBD Sector, the Royal Army Medical Corps and civil surgeons. This work was particularly important in the context of terrorist explosives. Blast injury research, aimed at elucidating the interaction of fast-riding pressure waves with the body and the possibility of designing improved EOD protective clothing, has been a major medical concern in the CBD Sector for some years, as has intestinal injury, penetrating head injuries and foot injuries. All these topics are also of prime interest to civil medicine.

Nerve agent prophylaxis and therapy

The administration of relevant drugs to protect against nerve agent poisoning and to negate the effects of nerve agent in the body after exposure has traditionally been achieved by, respectively, the self-administration of oral tablets of pyridostigmine (the Nerve Agent Pre-treatment Set (NAPS)) and self injection, using the Autoject Combopen, with atropine, pralidoxime and avizafone. There is a strong possibility that the self-administration of oral tablets could be obviated by the incorporation of prophylactic drugs in a self-adhesive trans-dermal patch which could be applied by the Serviceman when attack threatens and thus provide an even uptake of the physostigmine and hyoscine formulation, with none of the transient side-effects of oral ingestion of pyridostigmine. The development of more effective therapeutic therapies is also being examined.

Mustard gas, burn prophylaxis and therapy

As yet there is no specific prophylaxis for mustard gas burns, although several compounds have been identified as protecting tissue cells. Therapy for mustard gas burns is at present non-specific and research is centered on the pharmaceutical approach and on surgical intervention, such as dermabrasion. This is essentially a long term study in understanding the chemical pathology of the lesions and elucidating the best regimes for treatment. Models for mustard gas skin therapy are being examined. Barrier creams may provide some basis for slowing or nullifying the effects of mustard gas on the skin. Such creams are being formulated and examined to this end. There may also be potential here for thermal barrier creams intended to reduce the infra-red burning effects of explosions.

In vitro toxicology

This involves the maintenance of cells and tissues from human and animal sources in long-term culture in vitro (ie literally "in glass") to provide a means of evaluating the cellular basis of toxic effects of chemical agents, potential prophylactic and therapeutic drugs and, in fact, lethal or sub-lethal effects of any compound of interest to CBD Sector's customers. To a degree, the cultured cells may replace animal use and certainly will reduce the number of experimental animals needed for tests. The tissue culture systems enable the development of models for lungs, skin or eyes and the effects of deleterious substances can be determined by a variety of biochemical and microscopical techniques. The potential for mechanistic studies is enormous and a great deal of innovative research is conducted. Recently, the CBD Sector has published its initial research on the protective effects of hexamethylenetetramine against mustard gas toxicity and also the evaluation of barrier creams by the use of such in vitro techniques. The study of the biological effects of pulsed ultra-wide band electromagnetic fields has also been reported: such work is relevant to the possible hazards of emissions from mobile telephones and related Service equipment.

Detection of Agents

The ability to detect in near-real time the presence of chemical and biological agents in the ambient air is a major requirement in defence. Many chemical warfare agents are colourless, odourless and invisible in aerosol or vapour form as are all aerosolised biological warfare agents. Real-time detection enables the donning of respirators and other individual protection equipment, essential to preventing incapacitating or lethal effects.

The present priority need is to optimise biological agent detection. To this end, during the Gulf War of 1990, an interim system for such detection and Service operators trained at the then CBDE, were deployed in Kuwait. Since then there have been considerable advances in biological detection arising from Porton Down research and development. The world's first reliable biological detection system, the Prototype Biological Detection System (PBDS), is presently deployed in the Gulf area. Based on a standard four-ton Bedford Truck, several of the Mark II systems, developed in collaboration with Hunting Engineering Consortium, are operational. The system depends on initial non-specific detection of alien aerosol particles signatures from analysis of the shape, size and number of particles. This is followed by continuous-flow luminometer assay using the enzyme luciferase to discriminate between biological and non-biological origin particles and specifically between bacterial and non-bacterial particles. The latter category can include material such as seaweed spores, pollen and other biological detritus including harmless and naturally occurring bacteria to be found constantly in the air in varying concentrations. The detection of bacterial particles is then subject to further discrimination to specifically identify pathogens through antibody-based tests for pathogens such as anthrax spores, plague bacilli and certain toxins. Confirmation by use of the polymerase chain reaction and gene probes follows. The system is essentially an integration of a human and computer interface, operated by Servicemen of the new Nuclear, Biological and Chemical Joint Regiment trained by the CBD Sector, which also is responsible for the logistic supply of reagents for the system. An Interim Naval Biological Detection System has been installed in HM ships deployed in the Gulf area and the completed system is expected to be in service on completion of sea trials early in the twenty-first century.

Decontamination

The standard in-Service decontaminant in the United Kingdom is CAD, or Chemical Agent Decontaminant, essentially an alkaline solution of the chlorinating compound sodium dichloro-isocyanurate. It destroys chemical warfare agents by oxidative or hydrolytic reactions when sprayed or sluiced on contaminated equipment and vehicles. The CBD Sector has recently sought to enhance the properties of CAD by a microemulsion technique involving the incorporation of a solubilising agent such as sodium dodecyl sulphonate with butanol, toluene or cyclohexane, to ensure the greater effectiveness of the physico-chemical interaction

A field trial on the Porton Range involving a contaminated Challenger tank undergoing decontamination by a pressurised spray.

between CAD and agent at the molecular level. Trials with contaminated armoured fighting vehicles using pressurised sprays and CAM micro-emulsion on the CBD Sector's range have proved highly encouraging.

Protective Clothing Evaluation

The protection of the Serviceman's body by the in-service NBC suit and of even more effective suits under consideration or development must be evaluated by challenging the suit with chemical warfare agents in realistic battlefield environments. Traditionally, recourse has been had to tests with swatches of suit fabrics but this does not allow for closures, seams, the bellows effect of wearing, fit and the effects of wind-flow. Further, in the present day, evaluation of suits using volunteers exposed to agents is not permissible. A unique and new Porton Animated Mannequin System generally referred to as "Porton Man" has been designed. This robotic mannequin produced with the collaboration of Ogle TNO Safety Products can simulate operational activities such as walking, running and passive postures, is based on anthropometric data from a survey of Service personnel. It is a man-sized and shaped fibre glass shell, articulated at the shoulder, hip and knee, driven by an internal, motorised pulley system. It can contain, under the suit, up to fifty dosimeters for measuring any penetration of agents, both chemical and biological. "Porton Man" is held in a 100m3 chamber under negative pressure and with the environment computer controlled. Wind effects are simulated by fans. The data obtained is invaluable for fabric choice and suit design in providing the optimum NBC suit for the Services.

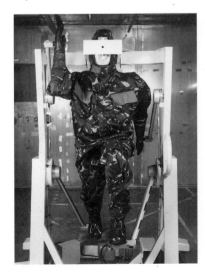

"Porton Man" in the 100 cubic metre exposure chamber.

Chemical modification of fabric and other surfaces provides a further opportunity for NBC suit optimisation. The surface properties of materials can be modified to afford specific effects, such as resistance to chemical warfare agents, water and oil-repellancy and improved liquid handling characteristics. The opportunities for chemically reactive coatings and membranes, innovative textiles and novel, air permeable barrier fabrics is being explored. Cold plasma technology is of particular interest. Plasma polymers can be deposited on a wide range of materials from radio frequency discharges. The concept of self-decontaminating fabric is attractive but complex. Reactive coatings based on a ruthenium catalyst have been shown to be active against mustard gas. The concept of novel, air permeable, barrier fabrics is being explored. The aim is to combine minimum physiological penalties for suit wearers with maximum protection from the penetration of agents.

Microbiology

Since the implementation of the enhanced biological defence programme in the early 1990s, molecular biology and recombinant-DNA work in the CBD Sector has been remarkably increased, notably in detection and rapid identification and in vaccine research. Vaccines are of paramount importance in protection against biological warfare agents. Although Servicemen have been immunised against naturally occurring infectious diseases since the early 1900s, no United Kingdom Serviceman received immunisation against biological warfare agents until the Gulf War. Although much vaccine research was done at the World War Two BDP, at the MRD and the later MRE, notably on protection against anthrax, there was never an operational requirement for Service immunisation against biological warfare agents until the Gulf War. Subsequently, the CBD Sector is researching the improvement of older vaccines and the development of new, through the opportunities engendered by modern molecular biology and the technology of recombinant-DNA. A highly professional group has emerged in the Sector which is now investigating the use of the bacterium Salmonella typhimuruim and adenoviruses as vaccine vectors, notably in association with the prospect of vaccines to be delivered intra-nasally or orally against plague, glanders and clostridial toxins. Oral immunisation is logistically attractive, provided that the problem of vaccine destruction in the stomach can be obviated. Here the prospects for micro-encapsulation of vaccines are being explored. In the Biomedical Sciences Department, molecular biology bacteriology, immunology, protein biochemistry, aerobiology, are all being coordinated to serve detection and identification needs, vaccine studies and diverse problems concerned with anthrax, smallpox, glanders, plague, other infectious diseases and botulinum toxin, identified as prime biological warfare agents. After the closure of the MRE and the devolution of a biological defence to a minimalised biological defence Division at the then CDE in 1979, the CBD Sector now possesses a large and effective multi-disciplinary microbiological element, with proper facilities. In 2000 this will be further enhanced by the opening of the Henderson Building, containing the most modern containment laboratory suites for safe handling of pathogenic microorganisms at Classes 3 and 4, as defined by the Advisory Committee on Dangerous Pathogens. Porton Down has a long history, since 1940, in the safe handling of dangerous pathogens, clouded only by the sad death of Geoffrey Bacon in 1962 from plague at the MRE and the 1976 infection, with the virus of Ebola disease, contracted by Geoffrey Platt at the same establishment. Happily, Geoffrey Platt recovered fully from this infection. Today, the guidelines for research with dangerous pathogens are now formalised and are much more stringent than the practices of 1962 and 1976.

The Future: Perceptions of Continuing Requirements

8

It may seem presumptuous to contemplate the unknown years ahead. In an ideal world effective and verifiable measures of arms control would have obviated the need for much of the role of the Establishment decades ago, but we do not live in an ideal world; nor are we likely to. Since the 1930s, some nations which have ratified international prohibitions on chemical and biological warfare have with certainty used chemical agents and may well have used biological agents. In other nations, whilst there may not have been use, there is good evidence of the capability to use. Some other nations have still to ratify the relevant arms control agreements and a few nations remain who have never signed or ratified. In addition to the existing 1925 Geneva Protocol and the 1972 Biological Weapons Convention, the Chemical Weapons Convention which had been under negotiation over the last 20 or more years now exists and is in force. It is likely to be several years before all its states parties can meet all its requirements. Destruction of chemical agent and weapon stocks and of production facilities is a costly and time consuming process. Even then, the verification of compliance with the Chemical Weapons Convention is a matter of such complexity as to be likely to necessitate the continued existence of CBD Sector as the focus of necessary research and advice. Similarly, it is likely that in the future some verification provisions will be applied to the 1972 Biological Weapons Convention. Microbiological research and biotechnological activity capable of misuse is ubiquitous. Microorganisms and toxins capable of use as biological agents exist in nature, evoke naturally occurring disease (unlike most chemical warfare agents which do not occur in nature and have no alternative civil use) and are the subject of a great deal of study. Given this plethora of activity, the discrimination between innocent and civil activity, permitted biological defence research and prohibited misuse presents great problems.

Against the background of such verification difficulties, there can be little doubt about the case for maintaining effective chemical and biological defence as an adjunct to arms control, in order to provide a deterrent to any aggressor contemplating the chemical or biological warfare option. The Sector plays a major role in promoting the effectiveness of verification and, alongside arms control, maximising the effectiveness of export controls in this field. The 1990s have seen great emphasis on control of dual-use exports which could be misused for chemical and biological warfare purposes. Effective controls which do not prohibit transfers of such materials for peaceful purposes need sound technical advice for enforcement. The Sector is already playing its part in the fields of chemical and biological export controls. Inevitably, all these developments provide a sound rationale for sustaining the Sector well into the future.

The late Dr J F S Stone, a distinguished archaeologist and a sometime member of the staff of both major Establishments at Porton, wrote an appendix for Kent's "History of Porton". In this he expounded the thesis that Porton had been the site of evaluations of experimental procedures some thousands of years earlier. The prehistoric flint mines, stock farming and fortifications could all be seen as man's earlier exploratory study in industry, agriculture and defence. Stone continued his theme with the local gun-flint industry of the Napoleonic era and concludes "What more appropriate site could have been found in modem times to carry on such a tradition of experimental studies than in this central part of Wessex born of an old stubborn determination to resist and prevail? Yet no one could imagine for a moment that such a historical background in any way influenced the minds of the authorities charged with the choice and acquisition of this stretch of land as an experimental ground in the 1914–1918 war to meet and combat the German threat of chemical warfare". It is difficult now to envisage that the CBD Sector at Porton Down could discontinue the traditions of the last 84 years perceived by Stone, however fancifully, as stretching back into prehistory.

Because of the considerable military utility of chemical and biological warfare, the vulnerability of the military and civilian population of the United Kingdom to clandestine attacks and the particularly unpleasant hazards that would arise, it is certain that the CBD Sector will continue to be seen as an essential part of the national defence programme, whatever levels of arms control appear in the future. No doubt the Sector will suffer uncertainties and vicissitudes as it has in the past; opprobrium continues almost unabated, but we can be reasonably confident that in 2016, the centenary of defence at Porton Down, will find the Sector still active at Porton and continuing the traditions of service to military and civil customers which were first established in 1916.

Major international changes have arisen in the last decade, particularly in the former USSR and Eastern Europe. There are uncertainties about the future role and nature of the United

Dr J F S Stone (1899–1957) a celebrated Portonian who held senior posts at both the major Establishments from 1925 until his untimely death in 1957, when he was the Superintendent of Technical Administration at the Microbiological Research Establishment.

Kingdom's Armed Forces. These reflect a changing but not diminishing threat. World wide manifestations of proliferating capabilities for chemical and biological warfare reinforce the Latin motto "Cave" which has been carried on the Establishment and then the Sector crest since at least the 1930s. We must indeed continue to "beware" and respond to the technically challenging capabilities against which protection is required.

What is Chemical and Biological Warfare?

Chemical Warfare

A chemical warfare agent has to be deployed so that it is inhaled as a gas, vapour or aerosol (a suspension of microscopic particles in the air) or as liquid droplets intended to contaminate the eyes and skin (some gases and vapours may also exert effects on eyes and skin). Agents therefore exert effects on the body after entering by either the respiratory portal, the eyes or the skin. Agents which can exert profound effects through more than one of these portals will be particularly hazardous e.g. the nerve agents or mustard gas.

Not all agents are essentially lethal. Some, like the lachrymators (tear gases), are intended to harass and be a temporary impediment Others, like mustard gas are vesicants (blistering agents) whose effect may be profound enough to immobilise and hospitalise men for many weeks. Others, like the nerve agents, are intended the kill and can do so very quickly at minute doses.

Some chemical agents do not exist as a gas or vapour e.g. certain arsenical compounds. They are deployed as a powders, as aerosols or as particulate smoke. Others exist as a liquid which gradually vaporises to a gas; here both the liquid and the gas will be toxic. A few agents can be released as gases from cylinders e.g. chlorine and phosgene. Most early chemical warfare was based on such use but this was soon superseded by the use of chemical munitions and other types of chemical weapons to deliver the agent directly on the target.

The purpose of chemical weapons is to maximise the dissemination of the agent on the target. The older cylinder method of dissemination relied on the wind to carry the gas to the target. Accuracy was limited by wind speed, wind direction, turbulence and the effect of terrain e.g. woods and valleys could cause diversions or delays. The danger of affecting areas outside the target, including friendly forces, was considerable. Shell, mortar bombs and aircraft bombs filled ("charged" was the traditional vernacular expression) with chemical agent could now be delivered on to the target by gun, mortar or aircraft with some precision. Wind direction was still important to obtain diffusion of agent within the target from the immediate impact area but chemical attacks were no longer critically dependent on the wind. The bursting of the munition on or over the target releases liquid droplets, aerosols or vapour (according to the nature of the agent and munition design). Chemical warfare is traditionally a tactical weapon for the battlefield but it can be used more strategically, especially by large-scale use of aircraft bombs or missile warheads, for attacks on rear areas, bridge heads, ports, airfields, the defence industries and, ultimately, civil populations.

Chemical Defence

The main aim of chemical defence is to protect the respiratory tract, the eyes and the skin. This can be readily achieved but troops would suffer some profound physiological and psychological penalties if they were to wear respirator, the NBC suit, NBC gloves and NBC boots continually, especially in hot weather. Such penalties would quickly affect fighting efficiency. The alternative is to know when a chemical agent hazard exists, so that the respirator and gloves can be put on. In the combat zone or highly vulnerable rear areas, troops will already be in their NBC suits, with respirators and gloves at the ready.

The approach of a hazard can be detected by automatic sensing of the air for aerosols or vapours, by battlefield intelligence, papers or paints which show by colour changes that agent droplets have descended from aircraft-borne sprays or air-burst weapons, by characteristic smells and other means. The ideal detector should run continuously and be remotely sited to alarm before the chemical agent reaches the unit, ship or facility that it s guarding and it should react in near real-time. Some detectors can also identify or discriminate between agents.

The protection given by the respirator depends on sealing off the eyes, nose and mouth areas from the outside air and allowing only agent-free air to enter the facepiece. This agent-free state is achieved by drawing the air through a canister containing absorbent charcoal to remove gases and fine filtration material to remove aerosols, smokes and other particulate agents. The NBC suit can also have absorbent charcoal incorporated in its air-permeable fabric or, it may be impermeable. Both concepts have advantages; the current British suit is permeable, the incorporated charcoal effectively prevents ingress of agent for a considerable period.

Prophylaxis against certain chemical agents can be provided by conveniently tabletted drugs to be taken in immediate anticipation of a chemical attack and immediate self-aid injection devices provide nerve agent antidote for unprotected personnel who have been unexpectedly attacked. Medical treatment can be highly specific or merely supportive. Often particular aspects of chemical agent poisoning can be treated by the armoury of drugs used in general medicine to relieve specific and life-threatening effects, such as lung oedema. Collective protection can be built into fighting vehicles, ships, command posts, aircraft shelters and field hospitals or indeed almost any structure. Here air is processed in much the same way as for the individual respirator but on a larger scale. Capital ships may also have pre-wetting systems designed to prevent residual contamination hazards from nuclear, chemical and biological attack by continuously wetting the upper works and decks to minimise adhesion. Residual hazards may subsequently be detected by hand-held monitors and extensive chemical and physical decontamination measures are available to neutralise and remove any intractable chemical agent contamination.

Biological Warfare

Biological agents are usually living micro-organisms e.g. bacteria, rickettsiae or viruses which cause infectious diseases. The term biological warfare is often taken to include the toxins; as does the 1972 Convention. Toxins, though not living, have their natural origin in certain species of micro-organisms, plants or animals i.e. their natural origin is biological. Agents are either liquid suspensions of live agents or solutions of toxins, or their powdered forms. Biological munitions and weapons create aerosols of the agent which enter the body on inhalation to evoke infectious disease, or for toxins a toxic effect. Not all such infectious diseases or toxic effects need be lethal; in the same way that few naturally occurring infectious diseases are lethal. Some may produce a temporary period of debilitation which will put exposed personnel out of action for a few weeks e.g. influenza, tularemia. Some toxins e.g. Staphylococcus Enterotoxin B may evoke a quick and transient debilitation lasting less than 24 hours. Other live agents or toxins may produce a largely lethal effect e.g. plague, anthrax, botulinum poisoning.

Biological weapons or munitions will be designed to maximise the dissemination of agent aerosol particle in the appropriate microscopic size range when the device functions. Munitions are likely to be aircraft cluster bombs or missile warheads, rather than artillery rounds. Other weapons are likely to be sprays mounted in aircraft, drones, vehicles or ships or portable static devices capable of being emplaced and deployed in highly clandestine ways.

Biological warfare is very flexible; no other method of war is capable of use on the same strategic, tactical and small scales to produce, by the appropriate selection of agents, effects which can be lethal or merely incapacitating, protracted or short-lived and fairly rapidly or often an incubation period of many days. A biological capability is likely to be much cheaper to develop than that for chemical warfare and the hazards and defence problems it evokes are likely to be more profound and complex. Further, the opportunities for clandestine preparations are considerable.

Biological Defence

Much biological defence is subsumed in chemical defence i.e. the respirator will prevent inhalation of any aerosolised agents and protect the eyes, and although the intact skin is relatively resistant to biological agents, the NBC protective suit provided added protection. The critical aspect of biological defence is to know when to put on the respirator or have recourse to collective protection. Awareness of a biological attack must depend on battlefield intelligence, aerosol detection systems, other inferential means and adopting a protective state when high risk situations arise.

Prophylaxis by immunisation is possible for most biological agents and provides a first line of defence, as against naturally-occurring infectious disease. Antibiotics and anti-viral drugs can provide further protection and therapy. Because of the vast number of putative agents, rapid identification of the agent is important for the selection of appropriate therapy. Most medical countermeasures against biological warfare reflect those used against naturally occurring infectious diseases. Not withstanding, most civilised nations may have had little recent experience of many such diseases, which may now be endemic only in remote areas.

Arms Control

The use of chemical and biological agents in war is prohibited by the 1925 Geneva Protocol. Most nations have ratified this agreement, either in the 1930s or after the Second World War, but largely with reservations that have effectively made this a no-first-use agreement. States parties have, however, breached the agreement on occasions in the past e.g. Iraq by use against Iran and alleged breaches are numerous. The Protocol does not prohibit the possession of offensive capabilities, merely their use in war. Many original States Parties to the Convention entered reservations permitting retaliation in kind and continued during the 1930s to maintain or acquire capabilities. The ability to retaliate-in-kind against non-signatories or even States Parties who saw advantages in breaching the Convention, was seen as fundamental need by most nations for many years.

The inadequacies of the 1925 Geneva Protocol in respect of biological warfare were ostensibly remedied by the 1972 Biological Weapons Convention which was intended to ban the acquisition of a biological warfare capability and to supplement the ban on use in the Protocol. However, the Convention still does explicity not prohibit possession of production facilities and has, at the time of writing, no provision for verification of compliance. As an interim measure certain confidence building provisions were agreed at the Second Review Conference in 1986 and finalised by a meeting of national experts in 1987. Substantial improvements to the confidence-building measures regime were agreed at the Third Review Conference of the Convention in September 1991 at Geneva. States Parties are now required to make annual declarations of biological defence activities and other relevant information, as well as a once-and-for-all declaration of past offensive and defensive programmes. The Geneva meeting also agreed a mandate for an international group of experts to examine the feasibility of verification provisions: the experts first met in Geneva in April 1992, when CBDE representatives played a prominent role. The slow move to verification continues.

A Chemical Weapons Convention, negotiated over a period of twenty years under the aegis of the United Nations opened for signature in January 1993. It finally entered into force in April 1997, 180 days after ratification by the

65th State Party. The Convention provides a global, verifiable ban on chemical weapons through a system of declarations and follow up routine inspections as well as more intrusive challenge inspections. The regime effectively underpins, for chemical weapons, the prohibitions on use set out in the 1925 Protocol. Since its entry into force, the Organisation for the Prohibition of Chemical Weapons (OPCW) set up in The Hague to administer the Convention, has carried out many inspections of industrial and military facilities world-wide, based on the declarations submitted to it by States Parties, CBD has to date received five inspections on the basis of its declarations to the Organisation. Work, in which CBD representatives play an important role, continues in The Hague to ensure the maximum effectiveness of the Convention". The Convention imposes controls over a range of chemicals, both chemical warfare agents per se and precursor compounds capable of use for the production of such agents, the so-called "Scheduled Chemicals". Many of the precursors have applications in civil industry and many companies and industries, and users, which produce these are covered by the provision of the Convention eg the chemical and agrochemical industries and the pharmaceutical industries. Any site which is capable of producing or using the "Scheduled Chemicals" is bound by the provisions of the Convention. They may be required to make annual declarations. In the United Kingdom the Department of Industry is the national authority responsible for implementing such legal requirements and lodging them with the international body, the OPCW. International inspectors from the OPCW may have access to sites at short notice, either regularly or on even shorter notice "challenge" inspections.

Trade in the "Scheduled Chemicals" between nations which have ratified the Convention and those which have not is controlled and, in some cases, prohibited. Under the British Chemical Weapons Act 1996, British industry which produces, processes or uses more than an explicit quantity of the "Scheduled Chemicals" are affected. The "Scheduled Chemicals" are of three categories. Schedule 1 chemicals are relevant if more than 100 grams are involved. This Schedule includes the nerve agents, mustard gases of several sorts, the lewisite series, the nitrogen mustards and saxitoxin and ricin, as well as several precursors. Schedule 2 chemicals includes Amiton, PFIB and BZ and a large range of precursors at the metric tonne level. Schedule 3 includes phosgene, cyanogen chloride, hydrogen cyanide and chloropicrin, all of which are putative chemical warfare agents but which have considerable civil industry utility. It also includes a large number of toxic precursors with industrial uses. The explicit quantities of Schedule 3 chemicals which determine inclusion is 30 metric tonnes.

The Sector provides advice to the DTI, the OPCW and, on a consultancy basis, to involved firms, to include evaluation of declaration requirements, assistance with completion of declarations, planning to receive internationally conducted inspections, risk assessment regarding the loss of confidential business information and its protection during inspections, advice on international trading issues and a variety of other relevant matters. CDE and later CBDE were the main technical advisers to the United Kingdom during the years of negotiation of the CWC. The Sector continues in this role in implementation, both for the government and to British Industry. The CWC is of considerable complexity and cannot be readily summarised here. This Convention has an intrusive verification regime and should, for chemical weapons, effectively underpin the prohibitions on use set out in the 1925 Protocol. The aim of the Convention is to provide a comprehensive, effectively verifiable and global ban on chemical weapons.

Under the United Nations Security Council Resolution 687 of April 1991, Iraq was obliged to accept the destruction of all its chemical and biological (and nuclear) weapons and all associated research and development, and undertake not to develop these weapons in the future. Since 1991 UNSCOM destroyed a considerable quantity of missiles, chemical weapons, bulk chemical agents and precursors, and CW and BW-related facilities. There are still major discrepancies and Iraq has sought to conceal many facets of its programmes and has ceased cooperation with UNSCOM. Operation DESERT FOX in December instituted during 1998 was instigated by the US and the United Kingdom to destroy Iraq's ability to revitalise its CW and BW capability. Iraq has not fulfilled its obligations under the United Nations Security Council resolution of 1991 and remains a significant threat.

In 1999 the CBD Sector achieved the status of a Designated Laboratory under the Chemical Weapons Convention. It is thus one of the twelve laboratories in the world authorised as competent to analyse chemical samples taken during inspections under the CWC.

A Selected Bibliography on Porton Down

The number of literary sources with information on chemical an biological warfare is vast and comprises official papers in the Public Record Office as well as books, articles and papers in learned journals by unofficial authors. Many such sources may have information about Porton Down, especially if they are works on chemical and biological warfare in the United Kingdom, but they are too numerous to cite here. Some information from unofficial sources may be speculative or even inaccurate. Also, readers need to note that official openness and transparency about chemical and biological warfare has not been a long-standing tradition in the United Kingdom. This can be seen in the 1975 "Scope" article listed below which, in a brief history of the MRE and its precursors, fails to mention the Gruinard Island trials of World War II and gives no glimpse of these offensively orientated field trials. By the 1992 "RUSI Journal" paper on BW and biological defence in the United Kingdom 1940–1979, the role of Gruinard Island and the wartime policy to develop a retaliatory BW capability are made plain. Equally, the 1992 book "Porton Down: 75 years of chemical and biological research" whilst listing the BW sea trials of the 1940s-1950s does not identify the agents used on those occasions. By the 1999 publication of "Cold War, Hot Science: applied research in the UK's defence research laboratories 1945–90" its Chapter 11 gives the identity of the agents, as does this present book. This slow burgeoning of openness has been almost overtaken by releases in the PRO and other areas of the public domain, which have seen recent massive releases of official reports from the two onetime Porton Down Establishments, particularly when public and parliamentary unease has been evident on specific topics, such as the CDEE field trials in the 1950s with zinc cadmium sulphide aerosol dissemination and the later dissemination of live harmless bacteria by MRE. Essentially, the late 1990s have seen remarkable openness about Porton's past and past UK policy in these topics.

This bibliography is almost limited to sources that provide substantial content on Porton's past: it is not a bibliography of sources on chemical and biological warfare and their defence. A bibliography of more general sources follows this selected bibliography.

The Royal Engineers Experimental Station, Porton
Lt Col A W Crossley RE (1919)
Public Record Office: WO 142/264

Report of the Secretary of the Chemical Warfare Committee for the period ending 31 March 1921
Public Record Office WO 33/987B

Second report of the Secretary of the Chemical Warfare Committee (1922)
Public Record Office: WO 33/1014

Fourth and fifth annual reports of the Chemical Warfare Committee (1924 and 1925)
Public Record Office: WO 33/1049 and WO 33/1078

Sixth, seventh, eighth, ninth and tenth annual reports of the Chemical Warfare Research Department (1926–1930)
Public Record Office: WO 33/1128, WO 33/1153, WO 33/1174, WO 33/1204 and WO 33/1231

Eleventh, twelfth, thirteenth, fourteenth, fifteenth, sixteenth, seventeenth and eighteenth annual reports of the Chemical Defence Research Department (1931–1938)
Public Record Office: WO 33/1272, WO 33/1298, WO 33/1330, WO 33/1359, WO 33/1389, WO 33/1443, WO 33/1484 and WO 33/1565

(This series of annual reports includes the headquarters branch for chemical warfare and defence within the Directorate of Artillery, the Master General of the Ordnance and the War Office, its experimental station at Porton, the process research establishment at Sutton Oak, extramural studies in universities and industry, and the Chemical Warfare (later Defence) Committee. These reports provide the most complete official account of events and attitudes from 1922-1938).

'The Microbiological Research Department, Ministry of Supply, Porton, Wiltshire'
D W W Henderson
Proc Roy Soc B (1955) 143 pp 192–202

A History of Porton
Lt Col A E Kent DSO MC RE (1960)
Public Record Office: WO 188/802
(This includes a preface written in 1992 which gives biographical details of the author)

A brief history of the Chemical Defence Establishment, Porton (1961)
Public Record Office: WO 188/785
(Written by C G Trotman, though authorship is not apparent in this booklet)

'The Microbiological Research Establishment, Porton'
C E Gordon Smith
Chemy Ind (1967) 9 338-346

'Porton's Story told'
G B Carter
Scope (May 1975) (a now defunct MOD Procurement Executive house journal)

Eight papers by CDE authors on several aspects of the Establishment's work in a special issue
Chemistry in Britain (1988) 24 No 7

'Microbiological war and peace'
C E Gordon Smith
PHLS Microbiology Digest (1990) 7 (2) 48–51

'The Chemical Defence Establishment'
The ASA newsletter 90–3 Issue No 18 (June 1990)
(In a series of articles entitle 'National Laboratories'; no author is shown)
'Gruinard Island returns to civil use'
Graham S Pearson
The ASA Newsletter 90–5 Issue No 20 (October 1990)

'A Tale of Porton Down'
Gradon Carter
Focus (1991) April pp 10-11 (The house journal of the Ministry of Defence)

'The Chemical and Biological Defence Establishment, Porton Down, 1916–1991'
G B Carter
RUSI Journal (1991) 136 No 3 pp 66–74

'75 years of chemistry at Porton Down'
G B Carter
Chemistry in Britain (1991) 27 pp 1095–1096

'75th Anniversary; the Chemical and Biological Defence Establishment (CBDE)
Porton Down: 1961–1991'
Gradon B Carter
The ASA Newsletter 91–4 Issue No 25 (August 1991)

'The Microbiological Research Establishment and its precursors at Porton Down:
1940–1979. Part I. Biology Department Porton 1940–1945'
G B Carter
The ASA Newsletter 91–6 Issue No 27 (December 1991)

'Part 2. The Microbiological Research Department and Establishment 1946-1979'
G B Carter
The ASA newsletter 92–1 Issue No 28 (February 1992)

'Biological warfare and biological defence in the United Kingdom 1940–1979'
G B Carter
RUSI Journal (1992) 137 No 67–74

The Old Portonians
G B Carter
The Royal Engineers Journal 1995 109 No 2 162–167

Past British Chemical Warfare Capabilities
G B Carter and G S Pearson
RUSI Journal (1996) *141* No 1 59–68

North Atlantic Chemical and Biological Research Collaboration: 1916–1995
Gradon Carter and Graham S Pearson
J Strategic Studies (1996) 19 No 1 74–103

Porton Military Railway
K P Norris
Industrial Railway Record
March 1997 No 148 281-295

British biological warfare and biological defence, 1925–45
Gradon B Carter and Graham S Pearson
Chapter 9 in:
Biological and Toxin Weapons Research, Development and Use from the Middle Ages to 1945: a critical and comparative analysis
Erhard Geissler and John Ellis van Courtland Moon (Eds)
SIPRI
Oxford University Press 1999

Chemical and Biological Warfare and Defence, 1945–90
Gradon Carter and Brian Balmer
Chapter 11 in:
Cold War, Hot Science:
Applied Research in the UK's Defence Research Laboratories, 1945–1990
Robert Bud and Phillip Gummett (Eds)
Harwood Academic Publishers, Australia 1999

A History of Microbiology at Porton Down 1940–2000
Peter M Hammond and Gradon B Carter
Macmillan, London 2000
(Accepted for publication but not yet published)

A General Bibliography on Chemical and Biological Warfare 1918–1999

This is not a bibliography of papers or articles but of books which are substantial texts

Auld, S J M
Gas and flame in modern warfare
George H Doran Co
New York 1918 (201 pp)

Warthin, A S and Weller, C V
The medical aspects of mustard gas poisoning
Henry Kimpton
London 1919 (267 pp)

Farrow, Edward S
Gas warfare
E P Dutton and Co
New York 1920 (253 pp)

Winternitz, M C
Collected studies on the pathology of war gas poisoning
Yale University Press and Oxford University Press 1920 (165 pp)

Underhill, F P
The lethal war gases; physiology and experimental treatment
Yale University Press and Oxford University Press 1920

Fries, Amos A and West, Clarence J
Chemical warfare
McGraw-Hill Book Co Inc
New York and London 1921 (445 pp)

Lefebure, Victor
The riddle of the Rhine: chemical strategy in peace and war
W Collins Sons & Co Ltd
London 1921 (279 pp)

Macpherson, W G et al (Eds)
The medical aspects of aviation and gas warfare and gas poisoning in tanks and mines

History of the Great War: Medical Services; Diseases of War Volume II
HMSO
London 1923 (621 pp)

Haldane, J B S
Callinicus; a defence of chemical warfare
Kegan Paul, Trench, Trubner and Co Ltd
London 1925 (84 pp)

Vedder, E B
The medical aspects of chemical warfare
Williams and Wilkins Co
Baltimore USA 1925 (327 pp)

Ireland, M W et al (Eds)
Medical aspects of gas warfare
The Medical Department of the United States Army in the World War:
Volume XIV
Government Printing Office
Washington 1926 (876 pp)

Foulkes, Major General C H
Gas! The story of the Special Brigade
William Blackwood and Sons Ltd
Edinburgh and London 1934 (361 pp)

Prentiss, Augustin M
Chemicals in war: a treatise on chemical warfare
McGraw-Hill Book Company Inc
New York and London 1937 (739 pp)

Liepmann, Heinz
Death from the skies: a study of gas and microbial warfare
Martin Secker and Warburg Ltd
London 1937 (286 pp)

Sartori, Mario
The war gases; chemistry and analysis
J & A Churchill
London 1939 (360 pp)

Thuillier, Major General Sir Henry
Gas in the next war
Geoffrey Bles
London 1939 (180 pp)

Hessel, F A, Hessel, M S and Martin, W
Chemistry in warfare: its strategic importance
Hastings House
New York 1940 (164 pp)

Wachtel, Kurt
Chemical warfare
Chapman and Hall
London 1941 (312 pp)

Waitt, Alden H
Gas warfare
Duell, Sloan and Pearse
New York 1942 (327 pp)

Bebie, Jules
Manual of explosives, military pyrotechnics and chemical warfare agents;
composition, properties and uses
Macmillan Company
New York 1943 (171 pp)

Fitch W K
Gas warfare: a monograph for instructors
The Pharmaceutical Press (The Pharmaceutical Society of Great Britain)
London 1942 (reprinted 1943) (103 pp)

Newman, Barclay Moon
Japan's secret weapon
Current Publishing Co
USA 1944 (223 pp)

The Chemical Corps Association.
The Chemical Warfare Service in World War II
Reinhold Publishing Corporation
New York 1948 (222 pp)

Rosebury, Theodor
Peace or pestilence: biological warfare and how to avoid it
McGraw-Hill Book Company Inc (Whittlesey House)
New York and London 1949 (218 pp)

Anon
Materials on the trials of former servicemen of the Japanese army charged
with manufacturing and employing bacteriological weapons
Foreign Languages Publishing House
Moscow 1950 (535 pp)

Brophy, Leo P, Miles, Wyndham D and Cochrane, Rexmond C
The Chemical Warfare Service: from laboratory to field
United States Army in World War II: The Technical Services
Office of the Chief of Military History
Department of the Army
Washington DC 1959 (498 pp)

Brophy, Leo P and Fisher, George J B
The Chemical Warfare Service : organising for war
United States Army in World War II: The Technical Services
Office of the Chief of Military History
Department of the Army
Washington DC 1959 (498 pp)

Rothschild, J H
Tomorrows weapons; chemical and biological
McGraw-Hill Book Company
London 1964 (271 pp)

Swearengen, Thomas F
Tear gas munitions
Charles C Thomas
Springfield
Illinois 1966 (569 pp)

Kleber, Brooks E and Birdsell, Dale
The Chemical Warfare Service: chemicals in combat
United States Army in World War II: The Technical Services
Office of the Chief of Military History
United States Army
Washington DC 1966 (697 pp)

Hersh, Seymour M
Chemical and biological warfare: America's hidden arsenal
MacGibbon and Kee
London 1968 (354 pp)

Calder, Nigel (Ed)
Unless peace comes : a scientific forecast of new weapons
Allen Lane: The Penguin Press
London 1968 (217 pp)

Watkins, T F, Cackett, J C and Hall, R G
Chemical warfare, pyrotechnics and the fireworks history
Pergamon Press
Oxford 1968 (114 pp)

Clarke, Robin
We all fall down: the prospect of biological and chemical warfare
Allen Lane: The Penguin Press
London 1968 (201 pp)

Clark, Robin
The silent weapons: the realities of chemical and biological warfare
David McKay Company
New York 1968 (270 pp)

(This is almost word-for-word identical with "We all fall down")

Brown, Frederick J
Chemical Warfare: a study in restraints
Greenwood Press
Wesport, Connecticut, USA 1968 (355 pp)

Rose Steven (Editor)
CBW: Chemical and Biological Warfare : London Conference on CBW
Harrap and Co Ltd
London 1968 (209 pp)

Report of the Secretary-General on chemical and bacteriological (biological)
weapons and the effects of their possible use
United Nations
New York 1969 (100 pp)

Cookson, J and Nottingham, J
Survey of Chemical and Biological Warfare
Sheed and Ward
London 1969 (376 pp)

Health aspects of chemical and biological weapons: report of a WHO group
of consultants
World Health Organisation
Geneva 1969 (132 pp)

McCarthy, Richard D
The ultimate folly; war by pestilence, asphyxiation and defoliation
Victor Gollancz Ltd
London 1970 (176 pp)

Thomas, A V W and Thomas, A J
Legal limits on the use of chemical and biological weapons
Southern Methodist University Press
Dallas, USA. 1970 (332 pp)

Stockholm International Peace Research Institute (SIPRI)
The problem of chemical and biological warfare

Volume I	The rise of CB Weapons	1971	(395 pp)
Volume II	CB weapons today	1973	(420 pp)
Volume III	CBW and the law of war	1973	(194 pp)
Volume IV	CB disarmament negotiations 1920–1970	1971	(412 pp)
Volume V	The prevention of CBW	1971	(287 pp)
Volume VI	Technical aspects of early warning and verification	1975	(308 pp)

Almqvist and Wiksell International, Stockholm; Humanities Press, New York and Paul Elek, London.

Neilands, J B; Orians, Gordon H; Pfeiffer, E W; Vennema, Alje and Westing, Arthur H
Harvest of death: chemical warfare in Vietnam and Cambodia
The Free Press, New York and
CollinsMacmillan Ltd
London 1972 (304 pp)

SIPRI
Chemical disarmament: some problems of verification
Paul Elek
London 1973 (184 pp)

Infield, Glenn B
Disaster at Bari
Robert Hale and Co
London 1974 (256 pp)

Robinson, Julian Perry
CBW: an introduction and bibliography
Political Issues Series: Volume 3 No 2
Centre for the Study of Armament and Disarmament
California State University
Los Angeles 1974 (34 pp)

SIPRI
Chemical disarmament: new weapons for old
Humanities Press
New York 1975 (151 pp)

SIPRI
Delayed toxic effects of chemical warfare agents
Almquist and Wiksell International
Stockholm 1975 (60 pp)

SIPRI
Medical protection against chemical warfare agents
Almquist and Wiksell International
Stockholm 1976 (166 pp)

Meselson, Matthew (Ed)
Chemical weapons and chemical arms control
Carnegie Endowment for International Peace
Washington DC 1978 (128 pp)

SIPRI
The fight against infectious diseases: a role for applied microbiology in
military redeployment
SIPRI 1979 (161 pp)

SIPRI
World Armaments and Disarmament: SIPRI Yearbook

      Yearly from 1968–1977 Almquist and Wiksell, Sweden
      Yearly from 1978–1985 Taylor and Francis, London
      Yearly from 1986 to the present Oxford University Press

SIPRI
World Armament and Disarmament
SIPRI Yearbooks 1968–1979: Cumulative Index
Taylor and Francis
London 1980 (89 pp)

Long, D
Chemical/biological warfare survival
Long Survival Publications
Wamego, Kansas USA 1980 (148 pp)

SIPRI
Chemical Weapons: destruction and conversion
Taylor and Francis
London 1980 (201 pp)

Sigmund, Elizabeth
Rage against the dying: campaign against chemical and biological warfare.
Pluto Press
London 1980 (120 pp)

Seagrove, Sterling
Yellow Rain: a journey through the terror of chemical warfare
M Evans and Co Inc
New York 1981 (316 pp)

Robert Harris and Jeremy Paxman
A higher form of killing: the secret story of gas and germ warfare
Chatto and Windus
London 1982 (274 pp)
(A paperback version by Paladin Books 1983 also exists)

The threat of chemical weapons: Spokesman Pamphlet No 78
Russell Committee Against Chemical Weapons
Russell Press
Nottingham 1982 (38 pp)

Beckett, Brian
Weapons of tomorrow
Plenum Press
New York and London 1983 (160 pp)

(Contains four chapters on CW/BW)

The Swedish National Defence Research Institute
Chemical warfare agents
Liber Forläg
Stockholm 1983 (57 pp)

Sims, Nicolas A
Chemical weapons: control or chaos?
Farnday Discussion Paper No 1
Council for Arms Control
London 1984 (18 pp)

Murphy, Sean; Hay, Alistair and Rose, Steven
No fire, no thunder: the threat of chemical and biological weapons
Pluto Press
London and Sydney, 1984 (145 pp)

Storella, Mark C
Poisoning arms control: The Soviet Union and Chemical/Biological
Weapons
Institute for Foreign Policy Analysis Inc
Cambridge, Mass and Washington DC, 1984 (102 pp)

Hamm, Manfred
Chemical warfare: the growing threat to Europe. Occasional Paper No 8
Institute for European Defence and Strategic Studies
London 1984 (47 pp)

Thomas, Andy
Effects of chemical warfare: a selective review and bibliography of British state papers. SIPRI Chemical and Biological Warfare Studies No 1
Taylor and Francis
London 1985 (125 pp)

Heyndrickx, A (Ed)
New compounds in biological and chemical warfare: toxicological evaluation
Proceedings of the First World Congress, Ghent 1984
State University of Ghent
Belgium 1985 (453 pp)

Perry Robinson, Julian
Chemical warfare arms control: a framework for considering policy alternatives. SIPRI Chemical and Biological Warfare Studies No 2
Taylor and Francis
London 1985 (116 pp)

Trapp, Ralph
The detoxification and natural degradation of chemical warfare agents
SIPRI Chemical and Biological Warfare Studies No 3
Taylor and Francis
London 1985 (104 pp)

McWilliams, James L and James Steel, R
Gas! The battle for Ypres, 1915
Vanwell Publishing Ltd
Ontario 1985 (247 pp)

Swedish National Defence Research Institute
Biological warfare agents
Liber Forläg
Stockholm 1986 (62 pp)

SIPRI/Pugwash
The chemical industry and the projected chemical weapons convention
Volumes I and II
SIPRI Chemical and Biological Warfare Studies No 4 and No 5
Oxford University Press
1986 (147 and 283 pp)

Perry Robinson, Julian
Chemical and biological warfare developments 1985
SIPRI Chemical and Biological Warfare Studies No 6
Oxford University Press
1986 (110 pp)

Spiers, Edward M
Chemical Warfare
Macmillan
London 1986 (277 pp)

L F Haber
The poisonous cloud: chemical warfare in the First World War
Clarendon Press
Oxford, 1986 (415 pp)

Stringer, Hugh
Deterring Chemical Warfare: US policy options for the 1990s
PergamonBrassey's
Oxford 1986 (76 pp)

The Swedish National Defence Research Institute
Biological warfare agents
Liber Forläg
Stockholm 1986 (62 pp)

Crone, Hugh D
Chemicals and society: a guide to the new chemical age
Cambridge University Press
1986 (245 pp)

   (Written by a leading Australian defence scientist, this has a chapter on
   chemical warfare and disarmament: the rest of the text provides further
   background reading which is highly relevant to an understanding of the
   problems of chemical defence)

Geissler, E (Ed)
Biological and toxin weapons today
Oxford University Press
1986 (207 pp)

BMA
The medical implications of chemical and biological warfare: a report of the
Board of Science and Education
British Medical Association
London 1987 (15 pp)

Trapp, Ralph
SIPRI Chemical and biological warfare studies No 7
Chemical weapon free zones?
Oxford University Press
1987 (211 pp)

Douglas J D and N C Livingstone
America the vulnerable: the threat of chemical and biological warfare
Lexington Books
Massachusetts and Toronto, 1987 (204 pp)

Gander, T J
NBC: nuclear, biological and chemical warfare
Ian Allen
Shepperton, 1987 (128 pp)

Moore, William
Gas attack: chemical warfare 191518 and afterwards
Leo Cooper
London, 1987 (262 pp)

Chemical weapons and Western security policy
The Aspen Strategy Group and University Press of America
Maryland 1987 (55 pp)

Hemsley, J
The Soviet biochemical threat to NATO: the neglected issue
Macmillan
London 1987 (163 pp)

Compton, J A F
Military chemical and biological agents: chemical and toxicological
properties
Telford Press
Caldwell, N J, USA 1987 (458 pp)

Sims, N A
SIPRI Chemical and Biological Warfare Studies No 8
International organisation for chemical disarmament
Oxford University Press 1987 (158 pp)

Cole, Leonard A
Clouds of Secrecy: The Army's germ warfare tests over populated areas
Rowman and Littlefield
New Jersey, USA, 1988 (188 pp)

Douglass, J D
Why the Soviets violate arms control
PergamonBrasseys
London, 1988 (203 pp)

Sims, Nicholas A
The diplomacy of biological disarmarment: Vicissitudes of a treaty in force 1975–85
Macmillan Press
London, 1988 (356 pp)

Lundin, S J (Ed)
SIPRI Chemical and Biological Warfare Studies No 9
Nonproduction by industry of chemical warfare agents: technical verification under a chemical weapons convention
Oxford University Press, 1988 (265 pp)

Hartcup, Guy
The war of invention : scientific developments 1914–18
Brassey's Defence Publishers
London 1988

(This has one chapter "The Ghastly Dew" on chemical warfare)

Piller, Charles and Yamamoto, Keith
Gene wars: military control over the new genetic technologies
Beech Tree Books
William Morrow
New York 1988

Williams, Peter and Wallace, David
Unit 731: The Japanese Army's secret of secrets
Hodder and Staughton
London 1989 (366 pp)

Spiers, Edward M
Chemical weaponry : a continuing challenge
Macmillan
London 1989 (218 pp)

Le Chene, Evelyn
Chemical and Biological Warfare: threat of the future (Mackenzie Paper No 11) The Mackenzie Institute
Toronto, Canada 1989 (29 pp)

Aroesty, J, Wolf, K A and River, E C
Domestic implementation of a Chemical Weapons Treaty
Rand Corp
California 1989 (126 pp)

Bryden, John
Deadly Allies
MacClelland and Stewart Inc
Toronto, Canada 1989 (314 pp)

(This is about early UK, US and Canadian collaboration in CW and BW)

Adams, Valerie
Chemical Warfare; chemical disarmament: beyond Gethsemane
Macmillan
London 1989 (276 pp)

Altman, J and Rotblat, J (Eds)
Verification of arms reductions: nuclear, conventional and chemical
SpringerVerlag, London 1989 (228 pp)

(Contains two chapters on verification of a chemical weapons convention)

Brauch, Hans Gunter
Military technology, armaments dynamics and disarmament
Macmillan
London 1989 (569 pp)

(Contains two chapters on CW/BW aspects)

Simon, Jeffrey D
Terrorists and the potential use of biological weapons: a discussion of
possibilities
The Rand Corporation
Santa Monica, California 1989 (24 pp)

Sinclair, David
Not a proper doctor
The Memoir Club : British Medical Journal
London 1989 (329 pp)

(A biography which contains two chapters on the author's WWII
RAMC Service at Porton and in Australia: both have interesting
historical information on CW/BW including the Gruinard Island trials
and mustard gas work)

Arnett, Eric H
New technologies for security and arms control : threats and promise
American Association for the Advancement of Science
Washington DC 1989 (341 pp)

(Contains six chapters on CW arms control)

Stock, Thomas
SIPRI publications on chemical and biological weapons: armament and disarmament developments 1968-88
SIPRI, Stockholm. Undated but believed to be circa 1989 (42 pp)

Adams, James
Trading in death : weapons, warfare and the modern arms race
Hutchinson
London 1990 (307 pp)

(Contains chapters on CW/BW)

Geissler, Erhard (Ed)
SIPRI Chemical and Biological Warfare Studies No 10
Strengthening the Biological Weapons Convention by confidence building measures
Oxford University Press 1990 (206 pp)

Stock, Thomas and Sutherland, Ronald (Eds)
SIPRI Chemical and Biological Warfare Studies No 11
National implementation of the future Chemical Weapons Convention
Oxford University Press 1990 (171 pp)

Utgoff, Victor A
The challenge of chemical weapons: an American perspective
Macmillan
London 1990 (273 pp)

Wright, Susan (Ed)
Preventing a biological arms race
MIT Press
Massachusetts, USA 1990 (446 pp)

Rogers, Paul and Dando, Malcolm
NBC 90: The directory of nuclear, biological and chemical disarmament 1990
Dfax Associates, TriService Press
London 1990 (147 pp)

Geissler, Erhard and Haynes, Robert H
Prevention of a biological and toxin arms race and the responsibility of scientists
Akademie Verlag
Berlin 1991 (501 pp)

Lundin, S J (Ed)
SIPRI Chemical and Biological Warfare Study No 12
Views on possible verification measures for the Biological Weapons Convention
Oxford University Press 1991 (124 pp)

Calogero, Francesco; Goldberger Marvin L; and Kapitza, Sergei P
Verification: monitoring disarmament
Westview Press
Boulder, San Francisco and Oxford 1991 (266 pp)

(Contains two chapters of relevance to CW and BW)

Picardi, A; Johnston, Paul and Stringer, Ruth
Alternative technologies for the detoxification of chemical weapons: an
information document
Greenpeace International
Washington DC 1991 (104 pp and appendices)

Cordesman, Anthony H
Weapons of Mass Destruction in the Middle East
Brassey's (UK)
London 1991 (224 pp)

(A RUSI Consultants Study which has sections devoted to chemical
and biological warfare developments)

Burck, Gordon M and Floweree, Charles C
International Handbook on Chemical Weapons
Proliferation
Greenwood Publishing Group
London 1991 (651 pp)

Papirmeister, Bruno, Feister, Alan J, Robinson, Sabina I and Ford, Robert D
Medical defence against mustard gas: toxic mechanisms and pharmacological
implications
CRC Press
Boca Raton, Florida; Ann Arbor, Boston, USA 1991 (359 pp)

Lundin S J(Ed)
SIPRI Chemical and Biological Warfare Study No 13
Verification of dualuse chemicals under the Chemical Weapons Convention:
the case of thiodiglycol
Oxford University Press 1991 (142 pp)

Bailey, Kathleen C
Doomsday weapons in the hands of many: the arms control challenge of the 90s
University of Illinois Press
Urbana and Chicago 1991 (158 pp)

(Contains three chapters on chemical and biological warfare)

Dahlitz, Julie and Dicke, Detler (Eds)
The international law of arms control and disarmament
United Nations, New York 1991 (234 pp)

(Proceedings of a symposium in Geneva 1991 and contains a few papers of relevance to CW and BW arms control)

ter Haar, Barend
The future of biological weapons
CSIS Washington Papers
Praeger
Washington DC 1991

Sur, Serge (Ed)
Verification of current disarmament and arms limitation agreements: ways, means and practices
United Nations Institute for Disarmament Research
Dartmouth Publishing Company, Aldershot, Brookfield, USA, Hong Kong, Singapore and Sydney 1991 (396 pp)

The Swedish National Defence Research Institute
A FOA briefing book on chemical weapons
FOA
Sundbyberg, Sweden 1992 (77 pp)

Herby, Pieter
The Chemical Weapons Convention and arms control in the Middle East
PRI0 (International Peace Research Institute)
Oslo 1992 (127 pp)

Krause, Joachim and Mallory, Charles K
Chemical weapons in Soviet military doctrine: military and historical experience
19151991
Westview Press
Boulder, California 1992 (247 pp)

Somani, Satu M
Chemical warfare agents
Academic Press Inc
London 1992 (443 pp)

Crone, Hugh D
Banning chemical weapons: the scientific background
Cambridge University Press 1992 (122pp)

Richter, Donald
Chemical soldiers: British gas warfare in World War I
University of Kansas Press 1992 (282 pp)

(Also published by Leo Cooper)

Roberts, Brad (Ed)
Biological weapons: weapons of the future
Centre for Strategic and International Studies
Washington DC 1992 (101pp)

Roberts, Brad (Ed)
Chemical disarmament and US security
Centre for Strategic and International Studies
Washington DC 1992 (158 pp)

Brletich, Nancy Runci, Tracey, Mary Frances and Dashiell, Thomas R
Worldwide NBC mask handbook
Chemical Warfare/Chemical and Biological Defence Information Centre
Edgewood Maryland USA 1992 (433 pp)

Latter, Richard
An end to chemical and biological weapons
Wilton Park Paper No 63
HMSO London 1992 (26 pp)

Zilinskas, Raymond A (Ed)
The microbiologist and biological defence research: ethics, politics and
international security
Annals of the New York Academy of Sciences Vol 666
New York 1992 (249 pp)

Shulman, Seth
Biohazard: how the Pentagon's biological warfare research programme
defeats its own goals
The Centre for Public Integrity
Washington DC 1992 (67 pp)

Wiegele, Thomas C
The clandestine building of Libya's chemical weapons factory : a study in
international collusion
Southern Illinois University Press
Carbondale and Edwardsville 1992 (199 pp)

Taylor, C L and Taylor, L B
Chemical and biological warfare : revised edition
Franklin Watts: Impact Books
New York, Chicago, London etc 1992 (128 pp)

Roberts, Brad (Ed)
The Chemical Weapons Convention: implementation issues
Centre for Strategic and International Studies
Washington DC 1993 (47pp)

Pechura, Constance M and Rall, David P (Eds)
Veterans at risk : the health effects of mustard gas and lewisite
National Academy Press
Washington DC 1993 (427 pp)

National Research Council
Alternative technologies for the destruction of chemical agents and munitions
National Academy Press
Washington DC 1993 (323 pp)

Smithson, Amy E (Ed)
Administering the Chemical Weapons Convention: lessons from the IAEA
Occasional Paper No 14
The Henry L Stimson Center
Washington DC 1993 (31 pp)

Covert, Norman M
Cutting edge: a history of Fort Detrick Maryland 1943-1993
Headquarters United States Army Garrison
Fort Detrick Md 1993 (118 pp)

Morel, Benoit and Olson, Kyle
Shadows and substance : the Chemical Weapons Convention
Westview Press
Boulder, Colorado and Oxford 1993 (345 pp)

Karsh, E, Navias, M S and Sabin, P (Eds)
Non-conventional weapons proliferation in the Middle East: tackling the spread of nuclear, chemical and biological capabilities
Clarendon Press
Oxford 1993 (300 pp)

(This contains one chapter on chemical weapons and another on biological weapons : some other chapters are highly relevant)

Brown, Mark
Public trust and technology : chemical weapons destruction in the United States
The Committee for National Security
Washington DC 1993 (12 pp)

Trapp, Ralph
SIPRI Chemical and Biological Warfare Studies No 14
Verification under the Chemical Weapons Convention: on-side inspection in
chemical industry facilities
Oxford University Press 1993 (114 pp)

Office of Technology Assessment
Technologies underlying weapons of mass destruction
US Congress
US Government Printing Office 1993 (263 pp)

(Contains two major sections on CW and BW)

Pringle, Laurence
Chemical and biological warfare: the cruelest weapons
Issues in focus
Enslow Publishers Inc
Hillside N J and Aldershot, Hants 1993 (104 pp)

(Written for "young people")

Poole, J B and Guthrie, R (Eds)
Verification 1993: peacekeeping, arms control and the environment
Verification Technology Information Centre
Brassey's (UK) 1993
London and New York (340 pp)

(Contains six papers on CW and BW related topics)

Findlay, Trevor
Peace through chemistry: the new Chemical Weapons Convention
Australian National University
Canberra 1993 (240 pp)

Deshingkar, Priyamwada; Meselson, Matthew and Robinson, Julian Perry
Antichemical protection and the Chemical Weapons Convention
Occasional Paper No 2 Harvard Sussex Program
Committee for National Security
Washington DC 1993 (71 pp)

Burns, Richard Dean (Ed)
Encyclopedia of arms control and disarmament
Charles Scribner's Sons
New York 1993 (1615 pp)

(Volume II of this three-volume work contains two papers on CW and
BW arms control)

Harris, Sheldon H
Factories of death: Japanese biological warfare 1932-45 and the American
cover up
Routledge
London and New York 1994 (297 pp)

Hayward, James
Shingle Street: flame, chemical and psychological warfare in 1940 and the
Nazi invasion that never was
LTM Publishing
Colchester 1994 (159 pp)

Bailey, Kathleen C (Ed)
Director's series on proliferation No 3
Laurence Livermore National Laboratory
California 1994 (64 pp)

(Two of the six papers are on CW and BW related topics)

Geissler, E and Woodall, J P
SIPRI Chemical and Biological Warfare Studies No 15
Control of dual threat agents: the Vaccines for Peace Programme
Oxford University Press 1994 (265 pp)

Dando, Malcolm
Biological warfare in the 21st century
Brassey's (UK)
London 1994 (258 pp)

Krutzsch, Walter and Trapp, Ralph
A commentary on the Chemical Weapons Convention
Martinus Nijhoff
Dordrecht 1994 (543 pp)

Spiers, Edward M
Chemical and biological weapons: a study of proliferation
Macmillan
London 1994 (249 pp)

A Royal Society Study Group
Scientific aspects of control of biological weapons
The Royal Society
London 1994 (125 pp)

Danon, Y L and Shemer, J (Eds)
Chemical warfare medicine: aspects and perspectives from the Persian Gulf war
Gefen Publishing House
Jerusalem 1994 (228 pp)

Bailey, Kathleen C
The UN inspections in Iraq: lessons for on-site verification
Westview Press
Boulder. Col. 1995 (151 pp)

Marrs, Timothy C; Maynard, Robert L and Frederick R Sidell
Chemical warfare agents: toxicology and treatment
Wiley, Chichester 1996 (243 pp)

Ranger, Robin (Ed)
The devils brew 1: Chemical and biological weapons and their delivery systems
Bailrigg Memorandum No 16
Centre for Defence and International Security Studies
Lancaster University
Lancaster 1996 (59 pp)

Kaplan, David E and Marshall, Andrew
The cult at the end of the world: the incredible story of Aum
Hutchinson
London 1996 (310 pp)
(Contains data on the Tokyo subway sabotage with Sarin in 1995)

Parker, John
The killing factory: the top secret world of germ and chemical warfare
Smith Gryphon
London 1996 (230 pp)

Thränert, Oliver (Ed)
Enhancing the Biological Weapons Convention
Dietz
Bonn 1996 (176 pp)

Cole, Leonard A
The eleventh plague: the politics of biological and chemical warfare
W H Freeman
New York 1996 (284 pp)

Brackett, D W
Holy terror: Armageddon in Tokyo
Weatherhill
1996 (206 pp)

Geissler, Erhard
Biologische Waffen – nicht in Hitler's Arsenalen: Biologische und Toxin-
Kampfmittel in Deutschland von 1915 bis 1945
LIT Verlag
Munster, Germany 1997 (304 pp)
(in German)

Barnaby, Wendy
The plague makers: the secret world of biological warfare
Vision Paperbacks
London 1997 (202 pp)

Price, Richard M
The chemical weapons taboo
Cornell University Press
Ithaca and London 1977 (233 pp)

National Research Council
Toxicological assessment of the Army's zinc cadmium sulphide dispersion
tests
National Academy Press
Washington DC 1997 (358 pp)

Roberts, Brad (Ed)
Terrorism with chemical and biological weapons: calibrating risks and
responses
The Chemical and Biological Arms Control Institute
Alexandria, Va 1997 (140 pp)

Stock, Thomas and Lohs Karlheinz
The challenge of old chemical munitions and toxic armament wastes
SIPRI Chemical and Biological Warfare Studies No 16
Oxford University Press 1997 (337 pp)

Eddington, Patrick G
Gassed in the Gulf: the inside story of the Pentagon CIA cover-up of Gulf
War Syndrome
Insignia Publishing company
Washington DC 1997 (347 pp)

Koplow, David A
By fire and ice: dismantling chemical weapons while preserving the environment
Gordon and Breach
Australia 1997 (354 pp)

Norris, John and Fowler, Will
NBC Nuclear, biological and chemical warfare on the modern battlefield
Brassey's Modern Military Equipment
London 1997 (112 pp)

Goodwin, Bridget
Keen as mustard: Britain's horrific chemical warfare experiments in Australia
University of Queensland Press
Queensland 4067, Australia 1998 (361 pp)

Sloan, Roy
The tale of Tabun: Nazi chemical weapons in North Wales
Carreg Gwalch
Llanrwst, Wales 1998 (103 pp)

Bunnett, Joseph F and Mikolajczyk, Marian
Arsenic and old mustard: chemical problems in the destruction of old arsenical and "mustard" munitions
Kluwer Academic Publishers
London 1998 (200 pp)

Mauroni, Albert J
Chemical-biological defence: US military policies and discussions in the Gulf war
Praezer
Westport, Connecticut and London 1998 (326 pp)

Proceedings of the Sixth International Symposium on Protection against Chemical and Biological Warfare Agents: Stockholm, Sweden, 10–15 May 1998
FOA-R-98-00749-862-SE
National Defence Research Establishment
Department of NBC Defence
S-901 82 Umeä, Sweden 1988 (410 pp)

Geissler, Erhard; Gazsó, Lajos and Buder, Ernst (Eds)
Conversion of former BTW facilities
Kluwer Academic Publishers
London 1998 (222 pp)

Endicott, Stephen and Hagerman, Edward
The United States and biological warfare: secrets from the early cold war and Korea
Indiana University Press
Bloomington and Indianapolis 1998 (274 pp)

Falkenrath, Richard A, Newman, Robert D and Thayer, Bradley A
America's Achilles heel: Nuclear, biological and chemical terrorism and covert attack
The MIT Press
Cambridge, Massachusetts 1998 (354 pp)

Sidell, Frederick R, Patrick, W C and Dashiell, Thomas R
Jane's chem-bio handbook
Jane's Information Group
Coulsdon, Surrey 1998 (298 pp)

Trevan, Tim
Sadam's secrets: the hunt for Iraq's hidden weapons
Harper Collins 1999 (448 pp)

Committee on R&D needs for improving civilian medical response to chemical and biological terrorism incidents
Chemical and biological terrorism: research and development to improve civilian medical response
National Academy Press, Washington DC 1999 (279 pp)

Schneider, Barry R
Future war and counter proliferation: US military responses to NBC proliferation threats
Praeger, Westport, Connecticut and London 1999 (229 pp)

Alibek, Ken (with Stephen Handelman)
Biohazard
Hutchinson, London 1999 (319 pp)

Defending against the threat from biological and chemical weapons
Ministry of Defence 1999 (33 pp)

Carter, Gradon and Balmer, Brian
Chemical and biological warfare and defence
Chapter 11 in
Cold War, hot science: appplied research in Britain's defence laboratories 1945–1990
Bud, Robert and Gummett, Phillip
Harwood Academic Publishers
Reading 1999 (444 pp)

Carter, Gradon and Pearson, Graham S
British biological warfare and biological defence 1925–45
Chapter 9 in
Biological and toxin weapons research, development and use from the middle
ages to 1945: a critical comparative analysis.
Geissler, Erhard and van Courtland Moon, John Ellis
SIPR Chemical and Biological Warfare Studies No 18
Oxford University Press 1999 (296 pp)

Regis, Ed
The biology of doom: the history of America's secret germ warfare project.
Henry Holt
New York 1999 (259 pp)

Lederberg, Joshua
Biological weapons: limiting the threat
MIT Press
Cambridge, Mass. 1999 (351 pp)

Hammond, James W
Poison gas: the myths versus reality
Greenwood Press
Westport Conn. 1999 (157 pp)

Index